COOKBOOK

Copyright © 2012, by Dana Luchini, CNT

Third print edition 11.11.2012

All rights reserved
No part of this publication may be reproduced, stored in a retrieval system, or transmitted by any means: electronic, mechanical, photocopying, recording or otherwise, without written permission from the author.

ISBN- 13:9781480298330

By: Dana Luchini, Nutritional Therapist

This book printed in the USA

Lose A Little or A Lot—Regain Your Health while enjoying delicious Lo-carb *Healthy-Aging Diet*™ meals

To achieve success on the Healthy-Aging Diet™ weight loss program, strictly adhering to the following food choice guidelines is a must! But it won't be a drag, because you have a variety of delicious food choices, flavors and combinations to choose from. To help you reach your weight loss goals, we offer our Healthy-Aging Diet™ cookbook. The 177 mouth-watering recipes yu find here will complement the hCG diet protocol and many other low-carb weight loss programs. Enjoy hot soups, creative salads, tasty desserts, sautés, dressings, sauces and more. You'll find meal recipes for Italian, Chinese, Mexican, lean meats, chicken, fish and much more!

IMPORTANT: DO NOT substitute any of the ingredients in these recipes!

HEALTHY CONDIMENTS

"I do believe that most condiments are killing us and making us fat!"

MCT Oil: This oil is listed in many of our recipes because it supports healthy weight and body composition. Medium-chain triglycerides are naturally found in coconut oil and are more easily and rapidly digested than other types of fats. MCT oil increases thermogenesis (energy expenditure) to help burn excess calories and promote weight loss. MCT isn't stored in the body as fat and doesn't increase serum cholesterol levels. It promotes satiety (the feeling of fullness) so you eat less without feeling deprived. MCT oil can be used effectively in recipes for cooking, baking, salad dressings, sauces & more. I like using an 8oz size with a sprayer for easy sprit zing on salads, pans. etc

Organic Low Sodium, Low Fat Beef, Chicken or Vegetable Broth: Be careful! High fat, high sodium broths sabotage your hCG weight loss goals. Find o*rganic broths* in the health food section of most stores. Never use anything but low sodium, low fat broth in these recipes. Add your own sea salt or liquid amino acids to boost taste.

Bragg Liquid Amino Acids: This vegetable protein seasoning from certified non-GMO soybeans is a great alternative to Tamari & Soy Sauce. Flavorful and healthy with sixteen amino acids, it's easy and safe to use. Use it as a marinade, on stir-fry's, dressings, sauces, etc. Purchased it at most health food stores or online. I like using the 6 oz size: I spray it on foods for additional flavor! Buy the larger size for refills.

Bragg Apple Cider Vinegar (ACV): Organic, raw, unfiltered, high in potassium and protein enzymes the benefits of this health drink are too long to list here; please read Bragg's book "*Apple Cider Vinegar Miracle Health System*". In a nutshell, **ACV** helps control and normalize weight & obesity, boosts digestion, elimination and detoxification (fights pathogens and body toxins). Essentially, **ACV** is an internal and external health tonic touted for its amazing natural cleansing, healing and energizing health qualities. *Bragg* also offers healthy seasonings: *Sprinkle, Nutritional Yeast & Sea Kelp Delight!*

Natural Sweeteners- Stevia, Xylitol & Lakanto: All natural sugar substitutes should be used with caution and in moderation! And even these have inconsistencies because they're processed by inferior companies that cut corners. So check your sources!

Stevia: a natural herb from South America called Ka'a He'ê. It's a sweet herb which has been consumed for centuries by the Guarani tribes. It's safety is legendary, too. The *Stevia* leaf is thirty times sweeter than sugar, contains no calories or carbohydrates, and is available in many flavors.

Xylitol: a naturally-occurring sweetener found in birch wood, berries, fruit, vegetables and mushrooms. In fact, the average-size adult normal metabolism manufactures up to fifteen grams of xylitol daily. *Xylitol* is classified broadly as a carbohydrate and more narrowly as a polyol or sugar alcohol, but *xylitol* is considered a "sugar-free" sweetener. While *xylitol* is just as sweet as table sugar (sucrose), it has about 40% fewer calories and 75% fewer carbohydrates. The body doesn't require insulin to metabolize *xylitol* so it won't raise your blood sugar the way regular sugar does, which puts tremendous strain on your system and causes negative health effects. *Xylitol* has been proven to inhibit the growth of bacteria so helps reduce the risk of tooth decay. Studies show that stevia's effects on teeth are long-lasting (possibly permanent); low decay rates persist years after trials are over. In addition to starving harmful bacteria of their food source, using *xylitol* raises the pH level of the saliva in your mouth. When pH levels exceed 7, the calcium and phosphate salts in your saliva begin to rebuild enamel where its lacking. For this reason, using *xylitol* (toothpaste, gum, etc) has shown a dramatic reduction in new tooth decay and the arrest and some reversal of existing cavities. While products made with *Xylitol* are beneficial to humans, be aware that—like chocolate, coffee, and grapes—*Xylitol* is toxic,deadly to your dogs and should never be fed to your pets!

Lakanto was developed in 1996 by SARAYA Corporation, the Japanese leader in environmentally-safe cleaning products made with coconut oil. *Lakanto* is great for baking and coffee; it has no aftertaste. Lakanto is a proprietary blend of two natural ingredients: **Luo Han Guo** fruit extract and **Erythritol. Luo Han Guo** is the fruit of the Siraitia grosvenorii vine which is native to Northern Thailand and China. The fruit extract is 300 times sweeter than sugar and has been used in China as a natural sweetener for nearly a millennium. In Traditional Chinese Medicine (TCM), luo ha guo has been used to treat constipation, diabetes, obesity, chronic cough and sore throat. It has also been used to promote longevity (hence its nickname '**The Longevity Fruit**'). It is reported to have strong antioxidant, anti-carcinogenic, glucose-lowering, immune-enhancing and Epstein-Barr virus inhibiting properties. *Erythritol* is a naturally-occurring sugar alcohol found in grapes, pears, melons, mushrooms and fermented foods (wine, beer, cheese, and soy sauce). While SARAYA derives its *Erythritol* from non-GMO certified corn, people with corn allergies should be careful (watch for itching and/or hives). *Erythritol* is used in sugar-free gum, low-carb foods, diabetic foods; some stevia sweeteners contain *erythritol*. It is about 70% as sweet as table sugar, ranks zero on the glycemic index, almost no calories, and taste similar to table sugar with no bitter aftertaste. *Lakanto* has zero calories and ranks zero on the glycemic index so it has no influence on blood sugar or insulin. It has zero additives, colorants, or preservatives and tastes smells and looks like sugar. 100% natural, vegan and safe for diabetics, hypoglycemics, kids, and overweight people. It doesn't feed harmful yeast (candida) and/or bacteria and won't cause cavities or contribute to tooth decay; it doesn't promote aging and/or suppress the immune system. It's easy to measure and use because it has a one-to-one ratio with sugar. It doesn't absorb moisture so it won't harden with age. Please _**remember, NEVER substitute natural sweeteners**_ (**Splenda®, Sweet N Lo®, Sucralose or any artificial sweeteners containing Aspartame**): these are toxic to your system and extremely contraindicated for any Healthy-Aging Diet™. Also eliminate **High Fructose Corn Syrup** or any "**corn syrup**" because they wreak havoc on your system and are made with genetically-modified corn.

Butter Buds: Use these fat-, gluten- and cholesterol-free butter-flavored granules in place of butter, margarine andoil. *Butter Buds* contain maltodextrin (a natural carbohydrate derived from corn), natural butter flavor (extracted from butter oils then dried to a powder-like form), salt, dehydrated butter, guar gum and baking soda. *Butter Buds* contain five calories per serving. Each serving (one teaspoon) is equivalent in flavor to two teaspoons of butter or margarine which contains 67 calories and eight grams of fat. The *Butter Buds* website reports these are all-natural, with no artificial flavors, no preservatives, no-fat or low-fat, no cholesterol, non-GMO, no trans fats, no saturated fats and Kosher (U). Warming up MCT Oil in a pan and adding *Butter Buds* opens the door for all kinds of tasty dishes. One unique thing about the MCT Oil is it has no taste but will take on the flavor of whatever you add to it. *Butter Buds* are available in the spice section of most food & health stores but can be purchased direct online at www.butterbuds.com

Miracle Noodles: These are made of naturally water-soluble fiber. They contain no fat, sugar, or starch and offer zero net carbohydrates and calories. They're gluten-free and made of a healthy natural fiber called Glucomannan. They're also wheat-free and kosher and easily absorb the flavors of any soup, dish, or sauce. They are instant, come in a variety of styles (angel hair pasta, orzo and rice) and have shown beneficial effects backed by medical studies for Type II Diabetes, Constipation, Obesity, and Cholesterol. Visit www.miraclenoodle.com for more information. You can include *Miracle Noodles* in many of the recipes you find in this cookbook. But please be aware that NET zero carbohydrates means they have some carbohydrates in them! So please use them sparingly your desired weight loss stalls. Most find that adding *Miracle Noodles* to a recipe adds to the flavor of the recipe and causes no weight gain; others say the opposite. So add to stir fry's, soups, sauces, etc. to form your own opinion of them. *Miracle Noodles* a bit of a fishy smell which can be removed by rinsing and patting them dry. Used in moderation, they should cause no problems.

Herbs & Spices: Use herbs & spices liberally in recipes to satisfy your taste buds. They they may even include some health benefits. Use fresh herbs as often as possible.

Hot peppers: Just about any type of (NON-PICKLED) hot pepper can be used in our recipes depending on your likes and taste.

Mrs. Dash: Mrs. Dash seasoning blends are natural blends of herbs & spices.

Sea Salt: Most of us grew up with Morton's table salt. I has sodium and iodine (good for thyroid) but the manufacturing process removes all the great minerals which are so important for your body. So use Sea Salts (I like www.Real Salt.com) with Sodium Chloride, calcium, potassium, sulphur, magnesium, iron, phosphorous, iodine, manganese, copper and zinc. Redmond's Real Salt brand also offers a variety of organic seasonings without MSG!

For a Healthy Life, Avoid the Following At All Costs!

Nonfat and Low Fat Products added corn starch and modified food starch, which is a carbohydrate! I'm finding this in dairy products and packaged lunch meats. Who wants a carbohydrate in your meat? Whole fat dairy offers saturated fat which helps you feel full longer and satisfied longer! We never the rampant heart disease in the early 1900's when we ate off farms, which included whole cheeses, eggs, milk, even though families cooked with lard! Fats are good for you!

Genetically Modified Foods: In the April/May 2012 issue of Green American, which focuses primarily on GMOs and the harm they are causing, they interview IRT's executive director Jeffrey M. Smith. Here are some excerpts:

Jeffrey Smith: "When I speak to doctors around the country, they report seeing an increase in the incidence and severity of certain diseases, which they believe are GMO-related. Moreover, when these doctors take people off of GMO diets, they report that the symptoms - of migraines, gastro-intestinal disorders, weight problems, and more - start to disappear.

GA/Tracy: *Can you give some examples of the troublesome studies?*

Jeffrey Smith: "The animal feeding studies for reproductive dysfunctions are astounding. Rodents that eat GM soy had changes in young sperm cells. Their testicles turned from pink to blue. The DNA function in the embryo offspring changed. In one study where female rats were fed GM soy, more than half of their babies died within three weeks, compared to a ten percent death rate in those fed non-GMO soy. The survivors from the GMO-fed group were largely infertile. In another, most hamsters fed GMOs lost the ability to have babies by the third generation. Infant mortality was also at four to five times the rate of non-GMO eaters. Mice fed GMO corn had smaller and fewer babies. This is just one topic."

"GMO Myths and Truths," published in June, smashes the claims from GMO lobbyists that anti-GMO arguments are emotional and anti-science. The genetic engineers authoring the study found just the opposite – there are sound scientific reasons to be wary of GM foods and crops and confirms the creation of toxins and allergens in GM crops as well as an adverse effect on nutritional value.
Dr John Fagan, a co-author of the report and former genetic engineer, said, "These

findings fundamentally challenge the utility and safety of GM crops, but the biotech industry uses its influence to block research by independent scientists and uses its powerful PR machine to discredit independent scientists whose findings challenge this approach." He points out that "Crop genetic engineering as practiced today is a crude, imprecise, and outmoded technology. It can create unexpected toxins or allergens in foods and affect their nutritional value. Recent advances point to better ways of using our knowledge of genomics to improve food crops, that do not involve GM."

Say Goodbye to MSG, all artificial sweeteners and corn syrups (see list above). I look at white sugar and white flour products as poison and suggest giving into them only on special occasions! Remember: when you eat carbs, you crave carbs! If I'm going to indulge, it's going to be dark chocolate sweets! (Word to the wise: If you crave chocolate you may have a magnesium deficiency!)

When Choosing Canned Foods Avoid

Sugars, sodium/salt and words that aren't food-related! Find good canned tomato sauces with minimal ingredients on the bottom shelf (usually) at your supermarket. The labels should read water, tomato paste and spices, period! (I use sodium free and add my own sea salt.)

Eating Out

Most restaurants are good with special requests, so follow your food list!
Here are my recommendations:
1) No sauces on foods
2) Order charbroiled lean red meats, chicken or fish with steamed veggies!
3) Order salads with lean meats, chicken or fish (I love crab and shrimp Louie's!)
Remember, most of your calories are in dressings and sauces, so avoid them and use lemon and red wine vinegar instead or carry your own dressing with you!

Breakfast: Order only eggs or omelets! I order a veggie omelet with tomatoes and cottage cheese instead of hash browns and toast!

Subway: Order Oven Roasted Chicken Salad or Veggie Delight Salad. Add toppings for your respective diet (use vinegar or lemon as a dressing). Don't trust oils when you're eating out; ask if the oil they use is extra virgin olive. If not, pass on the oil or bring your own premade dressing.

Red Lobster: I love shrimp on a skewer with charbroiled chicken breast and broccoli. No butter!

Fast Food Restaurants: In a pinch, grab a beef or chicken burger but ask that it be wrapped in lettuce instead of bread.

Maintenance

So you've reached your target weight. Now you need to know how to maintain it for life! Your best oils are MCT oil, Extra Virgin Olive Oil, Organic Extra Virgin Coconut Oil & butter (no salt). Stay away from bad ingredients as much as possible to stay healthy! Now that you've learned to eat healthy, if you see your scale numbers going up 5-7 lbs during vacation or the holidays, immediately return to the food list to lose that water weight in just one week! But if you wait until you've gained ten or more pounds, you've fat on so, once again, follow the diet for a month without cheating! You can lose about 1/2 lb a day on a low-carb diet by eliminating sugar, fats and sodium and getting into a mild ketosis where you're burning fat and losing inches! I don't recommend a 500 calorie diet at all because your body will go into starvation and store mode and when you eat again, you'll put the weight back on—plus more! You **must** eat 850-1250 calories a day according to your body type. I also suggest eating balanced protein to complex carbohydrates every couple hours to balance your blood sugar. Find a reputable doctor, diet clinic or Nutritional Therapist to help you calculate your body's protein needs. Professionals can also follow your progress and help you stay motivated while giving you suggestions that boost your weight loss. Also keep in mind that most of the time when you have hit a plateau it's because your liver needs nutritional support; it must process the fat, toxins, etc!. If you're hungry, not in ketosis or NOT having a bowel movement every day, this will can significantly slow your weight loss! Contact a professional immediately for nutritional guidance!

The Recipes

I have tweaked many recipes over the years to be healthier. Rule of thumb: Replace Almond Meal for "flour" in recipes, Stevia, Xylitol and Honey for "sugar" in recipes, sea salt for "salt", Bragg Liquid Amino's for Soy Sauce and Worchester sauce, MCT oil or Olive oil for ALL other "oils" and the organic Extra Virgin Coconut Oil for baking & candy!

Dana's Favorite Teriyaki Turkey Burger!!!
Recipe on Page 39

Healthy Aging Diet® Shopping List

Protein List: **Veal, lean Beef, Venison, Bison, skinless Chicken or Turkey breast, any fresh white Fish, Tilapia, Sea Bass, Flounder, Sole, Halibut, Salmon, Lobster, Crab, Albacore Tuna packed in water or Shrimp/Prawns.** *All visible fat must be carefully removed before cooking, and the meat must be weighed raw.

Vegetable List: **Spinach, Chard, Zucchini, Asparagus, Beet-greens, Lettuce or field greens of any kind (Dandelion, Rocket, Radicchio, Cilantro, Basil and others), Tomatoes, Celery, Fennel, Onions, Radishes, Cucumbers, Broccoli, Cabbage, Cauliflower, Eggplant, Artichoke, Mustard Greens, Collard Greens, Chicory, Endive, Green Bell Peppers, Jalapeno Peppers, Kale, Green Onions/Scallions, Brussel Sprouts, Turnips & Summer Squash, Mushrooms, Snow or Snap Peas, Pea Pods, Bean Sprouts, Alfalfa Sprouts, Bok Choy, Bamboo Shoots, Jicama, Okra, Green or Wax Beans.**

Healthy Fats: **Avocado, Olives, Whole Greek Yogurt, Almonds, Cashews, Walnuts, Pecans, Pistachios and Feta, Goat & Mozzarella Cheese.**

Fruit List: **Apple, Orange, Strawberries, Blackberries, Raspberries, Grapefruit, Sweet Peppers (red, yellow & orange), Lemon & Lime.**

Table of Contents

APPETIZERS & SALADS 1
- Apple & Asparagus Salad 1
- Apple Coleslaw 1
- Asian Chicken & Cabbage Salad 1
- Canned Chicken or Tuna Salad 2
- Cerviche 2
- Chicken & Apple Curry Salad 3
- Chicken & Fruit Green Salad 3
- Chicken & Orange Cabbage Salad 4
- Chilled Asparagus Salad 4
- Cobb Chicken Salad 5
- Crunchy Apple Chicken Salad 5
- Hearts of Palm Salad 6
- Italian Green Salad 6
- Orange & Cucumber Salad 6
- Refrigerator Garlic Pickles 7
- Seafood Salad 7
- Shrimp &/or Crab Cocktail 8
- Shrimp &/or Crab Louie 8
- Spinach & Artichoke Dip 9
- Strawberry & Cucumber Salad 9
- Spicy Seafood Salad 10
- Tomato & Cucumber Greek Salad 10

DRESSINGS, SAUCES, AND MARINADES 11
- Apple Relish Marinade 11
- BBQ Sauce 11
- Citrus Ginger Dressing/Marinade 11
- Cocktail Sauce 12
- Dana's Guacamole 13
- Dana's Salsa 13
- French Dressing 14
- Grapefruit Vinaigrette 14
- Horseradish Marinade 14

- Hot Cajun Dressing 15
- Italian Tomato Vinaigrette 15
- Italian Vinaigrette 15
- Ketchup 16
- Lemon Pepper Marinade 16
- Liquid Amino Marinade 17
- Marinara Sauce 17
- Mustard 17
- Orange Tarragon Marinade 18
- Papa's Pesto 18
- Savory Dill Dressing & Marinade 19
- Spicy Orange Sauce 19
- Strawberry or Berry Vinaigrette 20
- Sweet & Spicy Mustard Dressing 20
- Sweet Orange Dressing & Marinade 20
- Sweet Wasabi Dip & Marinade 21
- Tarragon & Garlic Marinade 21
- Teriyaki Sauce 21
- Tomato Picante Dressing 22

SOUPS 23
- Asparagus Parm Soup 23
- Beef & Mushroom Thai Soup 23
- Broccoli Soup 24
- Celery Soup 24
- Chicken Broth 24
- Chicken Tomato & Cabbage Soup 25
- Crab Bisque 25
- Fennel Soup 26
- Hot & Sour Chicken or Shrimp Soup 26
- Minestrone Chicken Soup 27
- Mushroom Soup 27
- Quick Chicken Vegetable Soup 27
- Shrimp &/or Chicken Gumbo 28
- Tomato Soup 28

Turkey Chili	29
Vegetable Beef Soup	29
Vegetable Broth	30
Vegetable Ginger Soup	30

POULTRY ENTREES 31

Asian Ginger Chicken	31
Barked Apple Chicken	31
BBQ Chicken	31
Chicken Cacciatore	32
Chicken Curry	32
Chicken Paprika	33
Chicken Pesto	33
Chicken & Spinach Rolls	33
Chicken Taco's &/or Taco Salad	34
Chicken Tarragon	35
Chunky Crockpot Chicken	35
Dana's Turkey Sausage Goulash	35
Lemon Chicken	36
Middle Eastern Spicy Chicken	36
Moroccan Lemon Chicken	37
Mustard Chicken	37
Orange Chicken	37
Spanish Style Green Chili Chicken	38
Sweet & Sour Chicken	38
Szechwan Chicken & Cabbage	39
Teriyaki Turkey Burgers	39
Tomato Basil Chicken	40
Turkey Sausages & Patties	40

BEEF ENTREES 41

Beef Bourguignon	41
Beef or Chicken Fajitas	41
Beef Kabobs	42
Beef Stew	42

Beef Teriyaki 43
Corned Beef Hash 43
Corn Beef & Cabbage 44
Ground Beef, Chicken or Turkey Taco's 44
Hamburgers 45
Herbed Crock Pot Roast 45
Italian Beef & Veggie Rolls 46
Italian Meatballs 46
London Broil Strips 47
Meatloaf 47
Minute Steak 48
Pepper Steak 48
Sloppy Joes 49
Spaghetti & Meat Sauce 49
Stuffed Cabbage Rolls 50

SEAFOOD ENTREES 51
Asian Grilled Shrimp Wraps 51
Asian Shrimp Salad 51
Baked Fish 52
Baked Mahi-Mahi 52
Baked Orange Roughy Italian 53
Baked Tomato Sole 53
Blackened Fish 54
Broiled Lobster Tails 54
Broiled Scallops 54
Cajun Jambalaya 55
Garlic Shrimp Scampi 55
Grilled Shrimp on a Skewer 56
Italian Shrimp & Zucchini 56
Lemon-Orange Roughy Fish 57
Onion Caramelized Shrimp 57
Pan Seared Ginger Red Snapper 57
Poached Salmon Piccata 58
Poached Halibut Fillet 58

Sautéed White Fish	59
Shrimp & Asparagus Salad	59
Shrimp Creole	60
Shrimp Curry	60
Shrimp & Grapefruit Salad	61
Sweet & Sour Shrimp	61
Tilapia Taco's	62

VEGETABLES ... 63

Artichoke Italiano	63
Asparagus & Spinach Salad	63
Baked Rainbow Chard & Feta	64
Beet Greens with Tomato & Onions	64
Big Veggie Salad	65
Broiled Sweet Mini Peppers	65
Cabbage Soup	65
Celery with Salsa	66
Cabbage & Shrimp Salad	66
Chicory & Orange Salad	66
Fennel & Cucumber Salsa	67
Garlic Cabbage Salad	67
Italian Asparagus Salad	67
Mashed Cauli-Tatoes	68
Onions & Burgers	68
Pesto Tomato & Cucumber Salad	68
Radish & Cucumber Salad	69
Sautéed Garlic Spinach	69
Steamed Asparagus	69
Sautéed Cabbage	70
Sesame Spinach	70
Spinach & Strawberry Salad	71
Teriyaki Onion Topper	71
Tomato Marinate	71
Tomato & Green Pepper Salad	72
Tomatoes Grilled	72

DESSERTS 73
- Apple Cinnamon Chips 73
- Apple Custard Pie 73
- Baked Walnut Apples 73
- Broiled Grapefruit 74
- Berry Sorbet 74
- Coffee Ice Cream 74
- Caramelized Apple Pie 74
- Chocolate Covered Strawberries 75
- Dana's Easy Chocolate Candy 75
- Greek Yogurt A La Fruit 76
- Homemade Applesauce with Cinnamon 76
- Instant Blender Frozen Yogurt 76
- Protein Soda Shakes 77
- Raw Apple Sauce 77
- Strawberries or Orange Slices Dipped in Dark Chocolate 77
- Warm Berry Medley 77
- Warm Spiced Oranges 78

Key:

TBS = Tablespoon

tsp = teaspoon

c = cup

APPETIZERS & SALADS

Apple & Asparagus Salad

Ingredients
6-8 stalks of asparagus chopped
1 apple diced
4 tablespoons lemon juice and water as needed
¼ teaspoon cinnamon
1 tablespoon finely minced onion
Sea Salt and pepper to taste
1 tablespoon MCT oil
Stevia to taste if needed

Directions: Lightly sauté asparagus in MCT oil & lemon juice until just lightly cooked. Toss with finely chopped onion, apple, and spices. Add salt, pepper, and stevia to taste. Chill in refrigerator for 10 minutes and serve as a salad or hot as a side dish.
Makes 1 serving (1 vegetable, 1 fruit)

Apple Coleslaw

Ingredients
½ head cabbage
1 apple diced
2 tablespoons lemon juice
1 tablespoon apple cider vinegar
¼ teaspoon garlic powder
Dash of mustard powder
Dash of cinnamon (optional)
Salt and pepper to taste
Stevia or Lakanto to taste

Directions: Slice cabbage in very thin strips. Toss with lemon juice and spices. Allow to marinate for 30 minutes or overnight. Eat coleslaw or add apples and a 1/8 teaspoon of cinnamon to make an apple slaw. Leave out apple for just coleslaw.
Makes 1-2 servings (1 vegetable coleslaw) (1 vegetable, 1 fruit apple slaw)

Asian Chicken & Cabbage Salad

Ingredients
100 grams chicken breast
Shredded Cabbage

3 tablespoons Bragg's Liquid Aminos
1 tablespoon apple cider vinegar
1 tablespoon minced green onion
1 clove of garlic crushed and minced
Fresh grated ginger or a dash of powdered
Pinch of red pepper flakes
MCT oil (for browning)
Stevia to taste
Sea Salt and pepper to taste

Directions: Brown the chicken with MCT oil and lemon juice, 1 tablespoon Bragg's, garlic, and onion. Slice cabbage into fine strips. Steam lightly until cooked. Drain off excess liquid. Add chicken, ginger, salt and pepper and chill. Sprinkle with additional Bragg's if needed.
Makes 1 serving (1 protein, 1 vegetable)
Modifications: Add additional vegetables such as bell peppers and mushrooms.
Maintenance: Sprinkle with 1 teaspoon toasted almonds or sesame seeds & water chestnuts.

Canned Chicken or Tuna Salad

Ingredients
1 can Chicken Breast or 1 can water-packed Tuna
1/4 cup chopped onion
1 stalk celery, chopped
1/4 c chopped tomato
2 TBS MCT oil & ACV Dressing

Directions: Stir onion & celery into chicken or tuna and put over lettuce of your choice, top with tomato and dressing or make sand which with low-carb sprouted grain bread.
Makes 3-4 sandwiches
Makes 1 serving (1 protein, 1 vegetable, 1 fruit)
Maintenance: Add Swiss or mozzarella cheese

Cerviche

Ingredients
100 grams chilled cooked white fish, crab or shrimp
3 tablespoons lemon or lime juice
Diced tomatoes
 1 tablespoon chopped onion
1 clove garlic crushed and minced
Fresh chopped cilantro
Dash hot sauce
Sea Salt and pepper to taste

Directions: Steam the shrimp, crab or fish. Add lemon, onion, garlic and chopped cilantro. Stir in diced tomatoes and hot sauce. Chill and marinate the ingredients in the refrigerator. Traditionally Cerviche is not cooked. The citric acids "cook" the fish. This is an alternative to cooking the shrimp or fish. Modifications: Add diced jalapeno, add additional types of seafood.
Makes 1 serving (1 protein, 1 vegetable)

Chicken & Apple Curry Salad

Ingredients
100 grams diced chicken
1 apple diced
Celery diced (optional)
¼ cup water
2 tablespoons lemon juice
1 tablespoon finely minced onion
1 clove of garlic crushed and minced
¼ teaspoon curry powder or to taste
Dash of garlic powder
Dash of onion powder
Dash of cayenne pepper
Dash of cinnamon
Dash of turmeric
MCT oil (for sauté)

Directions: In small saucepan lightly sauté chicken in lemon juice until lightly brown, add ¼ cup water and spices. Stir well and simmer over low heat until liquid reduces to form a sauce and chicken is cooked well. Add water as needed to create the consistency you want. Chill, add chopped apple and celery or serve over a green salad.
Makes 1 serving (1 protein, 1 vegetable, 1 fruit)

Chicken and Fruit Green Salad

Ingredients
100 grams of chicken
2 or more cups of any lettuce or greens
Your choice of apple, orange, strawberry or grapefruit slices
Lemon juice from fresh lemon
Dressing made from your choice of compatible fruit (see dressings)
1 tablespoon chopped red onion
MCT oil (for browning)
Sea Salt and pepper to taste

Directions: Cook chicken with a little lemon juice, sea salt, red onion and water until slightly browned. Prepare and wash lettuce greens. Lay chicken slices on top of greens and top with fruit and a dressing made from your fruit of choice. Examples: Strawberry

vinaigrette, grapefruit vinaigrette, spicy orange dressing etc. See recipes for dressings, sauces, and marinades.
Makes 1 serving (1 protein, 1 vegetable, 1 fruit)

Chicken & Orange Cabbage Salad

Ingredients
100 grams of chicken breast
½ head of any kind of cabbage
One orange (3 tablespoons of juice and remaining orange sliced or in segments)
1 tablespoon apple cider vinegar
2 tablespoons lemon juice
1 tablespoon Bragg's liquid aminos
Pinch of fresh or powdered ginger if desired
Dash of cayenne (optional)
Stevia or Lakanto to taste (optional)
Sea Salt and fresh black pepper to taste

Directions: Marinate strips of chicken in apple cider vinegar, lemon juice and spices. Cook thoroughly browning slightly. Prepare dressing with 3 tablespoons of orange juice, Bragg's, stevia, black pepper, salt and cayenne. You may add extra apple cider vinegar if desired. Shred cabbage into coleslaw consistency and toss lightly with dressing. Allow to marinate for at least 20 minutes or overnight. Top with chicken and orange slices.
Makes one serving (1 vegetable, 1 protein, 1 fruit)
Modifications: Sprinkle with small amount of sliced almonds or sesame seeds.

Chilled Asparagus Salad

Ingredients
Asparagus spears
3 tablespoons lemon juice or ACV
1 TBS finely minced sweet onions
Spritz with MCT Oil
Sea Salt and pepper to taste

Directions: Lightly steam the asparagus & onions until tender. Marinate in juices and enjoy.
Variations: Toss with the marinade of your choice for flavor variety.
Makes one serving (1 vegetable)

Cobb Chicken Salad

Ingredients
100 grams chicken cooked and diced
1/4 tomato, diced
1 cup lettuce, romaine or iceburg
1/4 Avocado, diced
1 strip Turkey bacon, cooked and crumbled
1 TBS Feta cheese
1 TBS Black olives, sliced
1 tablespoons lemon juice or ACV
1 TBS MCT Oil

Directions: Top lettuce with remaining ingredients and dressing (ACV, Lemon & MCT oil). Makes 1 serving (1 protein, 1 vegetable, 1 fruit, 1 fat)

Crunchy Apple Chicken Salad

Ingredients
100 grams chicken cooked and diced
1 apple diced
3 stalks celery diced
3 tablespoons lemon juice
1/8 teaspoon cinnamon
Dash of nutmeg
Dash of cardamom
Dash of salt
Stevia or Lakanto to taste
Wedge of lemon

Directions: Mix ingredients together, sprinkle with stevia and cinnamon. Chill for 20 minutes. Serve with a wedge of lemon and enjoy.
Makes 1 serving (1 protein, 1 vegetable, 1 fruit)
Maintenance: Add almonds or walnuts

Hearts of Palm Salad

Ingredients
1 jar Hearts of Palm (Trader Joes)
Spritz with MCT Oil
1+ tsp apple cider vinegar (ACV)
Sea Salt &/or pepper to taste

Directions: Drain Hearts of Palm and rinse with cold water. Spritz with MCT & add ACV and seasoning to taste. Refrigerate/marinate for 20-30 minutes and serve.
Variations: Add chopped tomatoes (used as a fruit serving)
Makes 3 servings (1 vegetable)

Italian Green Salad

Ingredients
1 stalk chopped Romaine lettuce
1/2 cup chopped red pepper
1/2 cup cherry tomatoes
1/4 cup Feta cheese
¼ cup apple cider vinegar
1-2 tablespoon Bragg's liquid aminos
1 tablespoon minced red onion
Salt and black pepper to taste

Directions: Chop up lettuce. Add red pepper, tomatoes & cheese. In a small bowl, combine the liquid ingredients, onion & spices. Toss dressing mixture over salad.
Makes 2 servings (1 vegetable, 1 fruit)
Maintenance: Add Kalamata Olives

Orange & Cucumber Salad

Ingredients
1 cucumber sliced
Orange slices (1 orange)
Orange juice from 3 segments
1 tablespoon lemon juice
1 teaspoon apple cider vinegar
1 teaspoon fresh tarragon minced
1 tablespoon sweet onion minced
Sea Salt and pepper to taste
Stevia or Lakanto to taste
Chopped fresh mint leaves (optional)

Directions: Combine apple cider vinegar, onion, spices and mix well, add stevia to taste. Add cucumber and orange slices, tarragon, salt, and pepper to taste. Marinate for

30 minutes. Garnish with fresh mint leaves. Modifications: Spritz with MCT oil; top with roasted pine nuts or sunflower seeds.
Makes one serving (1 vegetable, 1 fruit)

Refrigerator Garlic Pickles

Ingredients
One medium cucumber sliced into rounds
4 cloves of garlic in thin slices
1 TBS minced red onion
¼- ½ cup apple cider vinegar
3 tablespoons lemon juice
Sea Salt
1 TBS MCT Oil

Directions: Mix liquid ingredients & onion together. Salt cucumber slices well. Pack cucumber slices tightly into a small glass canning jar layering garlic slices in between layers. Pour apple cider vinegar and lemon juice into container until liquid covers the slices. Refrigerate overnight. Pickles can be refrigerated for up to 4 days. Or marinate cucumber slices in salt, vinegar and garlic then use a pickle press or weighted plate to press out excess liquid.
Makes 1-2 servings (1 vegetable)

Seafood Salad

Ingredients
100 grams lobster tail diced or other seafood
Celery, sliced steamed fennel bulb, or tomatoes (optional)
Lettuce of your choice
1 tablespoon lemon or lime juice
1 teaspoon apple cider vinegar
Pinch of chopped green onion
Pinch of tarragon
Salt and black pepper to taste
Stevia to taste

Directions: Mix seafood, liquid ingredients and spices together and serve over a salad, greens, or with another vegetable.
Makes 1 serving (1 protein, 1 vegetable)

Shrimp and/or Crab Cocktail

Ingredients
100 grams bay shrimp and/or cooked crab
1/4 cup Chopped Celery
Cocktail sauce
3 ounces tomato paste
2 tablespoons lemon juice
1 tablespoon apple cider vinegar
1 tsp red pepper or
1/8 teaspoon of horseradish to taste
1/4 tsp onion powder
1 tsp Liquid Aminos
Stevia or Lakanto to taste
Water as needed for desired consistency

Directions: Mix tomato paste, vinegar, horseradish and/or red pepper, lemon juice and spices together and allow spices to marinate and dipping sauce to chill. Add additional water as needed to create desired consistency. Put celery in bottom of serving glass, add layer of sauce, add shrimp and/or crab and top with cocktail sauce. Chill for 30 minutes in the refrigerator. Makes 1 serving (1 protein, 1 vegetable)

Shrimp and/or Crab Louie

Ingredients
100 grams bay shrimp and/or cooked crab
1 cup lettuce of choice, washed, chopped
1/4 cup celery, chopped
4 spears of cooked asparagus
4 slices cucumber
1/4 avocado, sliced
1-2 lemon, wedges
1 tablespoon apple cider vinegar
1/2 hardboiled egg
1 TBS MCT oil

Directions: Top lettuce with shrimp and/or crab, put sections of celery, cucumber, avocado and egg on top. Pour dressing of choice. I like MCT oil and ACV with a squeeze of lemon over fish. Chill for 30 minutes in the refrigerator. Garnish with parsley.
Makes 1 serving (1 protein, 1 vegetable)

Spinach & Artichoke Dip

Ingredients
1 bag of frozen chopped spinach
1 can of artichoke hearts (Trader Joes)
¼ cup Romano/Parmesan cheese
3/4 cup Ricotta cheese
1 tsp fresh lemon juice
2 cloves finely minced garlic
1/2 cup mozzarella cheese
1/8 tsp ground red pepper
Salt and black pepper to taste

Directions: Thaw spinach, drain, squeeze dry. Rinse artichoke hearts in cold water and quarter. Stir in spinach & artichoke to Parmesan, Ricotta, lemon juice, garlic & seasoning mixture. Spray casserole pan with MCT & top with mozzarella cheese. Preheat oven to 350 and cook uncovered for 30-40 minutes or until browning. Dip with celery sticks, or any other veggie! Best during maintenance but gives you an healthy alternative for get-togethers! Makes 10-12 servings (1 vegetable)

Strawberry & Cucumber Salad

Ingredients
1 whole cucumber
Sliced strawberries
1 serving strawberry vinaigrette (See recipe)
Stevia or Lakanto to taste if needed

Directions: Slice strawberries and cucumber. Toss with strawberries, add dressing and stevia to taste. Allow to marinate for at least 10 minutes.
Makes 1-2 servings (1 vegetable, 1 fruit)

Spicy Seafood Salad

Ingredients
100 grams crab
Celery diced (optional)
1 tablespoon lemon juice
2 teaspoons apple cider vinegar
1 tablespoon Bragg's liquid aminos
1 tablespoon finely minced red or sweet onion
Dash of garlic powder
Dash of onion powder
Cayenne pepper to taste
Salt and black pepper to taste

Directions: Steam the crab or seafood and chop into medium chunks. Toss with onions, spices, and liquid ingredients. Marinate for 15 minutes or more and serve over mixed green salad or add diced celery. Makes one serving (1 protein, 1 vegetable)

Tomato & Cucumber Greek Salad

Ingredients
1/2 cup sweet cherry tomatoes or tomato wedges
1 medium cucumber
1/2 cup green pepper, chopped
1/4 cup sliced red onion
1/8 cup Feta Cheese
1 TBS lemon juice
1/4 cup apple cider vinegar (ACV)
1 TBS MCT Oil
Sea Salt and black pepper to taste

Directions: Dice tomato, green pepper & cucumber. Add onion. In small bowl combine MCT, ACV, lemon and seasoning, toss dressing mixture into veggies and top with Feta & olives if applicable . Can marinate for at least an hour or overnight. If you like you can spritz with Liquid Amino's for more flavor. Maintenance: Add black or Kalamata Olives. Makes 3-4 servings (1 vegetable, 1 fruit)

DRESSINGS, SAUCES, AND MARINADES

Apple Relish Marinade

Ingredients
1 apple finely minced
1 stalk of celery minced (optional)
2 tablespoons apple cider
2 tablespoons lemon juice
1 teaspoon minced red onion
Dash of Liquid Aminos
Salt and pepper to taste
Stevia or Lakanto to taste

Directions: Mix apples and celery together. Dissolve spices into liquid ingredients and pour over the apple mixture. Mix well and allow ingredients to marinate for 30 minutes or longer to allow flavors to blend. Makes 1 serving (1 fruit, 1 vegetable)

Barbeque Sauce

Ingredients
3 ounces tomato paste
¼ cup apple cider or red wine vinegar
3 tablespoons lemon juice
1 tablespoon red pepper
1 tablespoon minced onion
3 cloves garlic crushed and minced
¼ teaspoon chili powder
½ teaspoon Liquid Aminos
½ teaspoon garlic powder
½ teaspoon onion powder
1 teaspoon chopped parsley
Stevia to taste
Cayenne pepper to taste
Salt and pepper to taste
Water as needed to achieve desired consistency

Directions: In a small saucepan, combine all ingredients. Mix well and bring to a boil. Reduce heat and simmer for at least 5 minutes adding a little water to achieve desired consistency and to make sure it doesn't burn. Use as a barbeque sauce for chicken or beef. Makes 1-2 servings (1 vegetable)

Citrus Ginger Dressing/Marinade

Ingredients
1 tablespoon lemon juice

2 tablespoons orange juice
1 teaspoon apple cider vinegar
1 tablespoon Bragg's liquid aminos
Ginger fresh or ground to taste
Salt and fresh black pepper to taste
1 teaspoon MCT oil
Stevia to taste

Directions: Combine spices with liquid ingredients. Enjoy over salad or double the recipe for use as a marinade. Warm slightly to enhance the flavors. Serve with additional orange slices to complete a fruit serving.
Makes 1-2 serving (1 fruit)

Cocktail Sauce

Ingredients
3 ounces tomato paste
2 tablespoons lemon juice
1 tablespoon apple cider vinegar
1/4-1/2 tsp red pepper or 1/8 teaspoon of horseradish to taste
1/4 tsp onion powder
1/4 tsp celery salt (I like to add1 TBS minced celery too)
1 tsp Liquid Aminos
Stevia or Lakanto to taste
Water as needed for desired consistency

Directions: Mix tomato paste, vinegar, horseradish and/or red pepper, lemon juice and spices together and allow spices to marinate and dipping sauce to chill. Add additional water as needed to create desired consistency. Put celery in bottom of serving glass, add layer of sauce, add shrimp and/or crab and top with cocktail sauce. Chill for 30 minutes in the refrigerator.
Makes 1-2 servings (1 vegetable)

Dana's Guacamole

Ingredients
1 ripe avocado, mashed
Dana's Salsa (recipe below)

Directions: Mix 1/2 cup Dana's Salsa into mashed avocado. My Favorite for dippin's!
Makes 4+ servings (1 vegetable, 1 fat)

Dana's Salsa

Ingredients
1 cup fresh chopped tomato
1/4 cup diced sweet onion
1/2 cup diced celery
1 small can mild diced green chili's
1- 14.5 can organic low sodium/sugar free Mexican style stewed tomatoes
2 cloves garlic crushed and minced
Fresh chopped cilantro
Salt and pepper to taste

Directions: Puree ingredients in food processor for smooth salsa or chop ingredients by hand for chunkier salsa. Add spices and chill in the refrigerator for 10 minutes or more to allow flavors to blend. Modifications: Add chopped jalapeno or chipotle peppers. If you like it hot add medium or hot chili's! Dip with celery sticks!
Makes 3-4 serving (1 vegetable)

French Dressing

Ingredients
¼ cup low sodium beef broth
2 tablespoons apple cider vinegar
2 tablespoons lemon juice
1 clove garlic crushed and minced
¼ teaspoon horseradish or to taste
½ teaspoon paprika
1/8 teaspoon mustard powder
Cayenne pepper to taste
Stevia or Lakanto to taste

Directions: Dissolve spices in broth, vinegar and lemon juice. Mix well and heat slightly in small saucepan. Chill and serve over mixed greens or vegetables.
Makes 2 servings

Grapefruit Vinaigrette

Ingredients
Juice of 3 segments of grapefruit
1 tablespoon lemon juice
1 teaspoon apple cider vinegar (optional)
1 teaspoon MCT oil
Stevia or Lakanto to taste

Directions: Combine juices and vinegar together. Add stevia to taste. Pour over mixed green salad and top with remaining grapefruit segments. Use as a marinade for fish, shrimp or chicken. Add salt and fresh ground pepper.
Makes 1-2 servings (1 fruit)

Horseradish Marinade & Dipping Sauce

Ingredients
¼ cup organic low sodium beef broth
1 teaspoon of horseradish or to taste
½ teaspoon garlic powder
¼ teaspoon paprika
1 teaspoon MCT oil

Directions: Whisk the ingredients together and heat the sauce in a small saucepan. Pour into dipping bowl or use as a sauce or marinade and enjoy with beef dishes.
Makes 1-2 servings

Hot Cajun Dressing/Dipping Sauce

Ingredients
3 tablespoons apple cider vinegar
1 tablespoon lemon juice
Dash of garlic powder
Dash of onion powder
Cayenne pepper to taste
Salt and black pepper to taste
1 tablespoon MCT oil
1 tsp liquid aminos

Directions: Combine ingredients in small bowl and pour over salad. You can also serve this as a dipping sauce or marinade for vegetables or fish.
Makes 1-2 servings

Italian Tomato Vinaigrette

Ingredients
3 tablespoons tomato paste
3 tablespoons apple cider vinegar
2 tablespoons lemon juice
¼ cup water, low sodium chicken or vegetable broth
1 tablespoon minced onion
½ teaspoon garlic powder
½ teaspoon onion powder
1 teaspoon dried basil or fresh rolled and sliced basil leaves to taste
1/8 teaspoon oregano
1 tablespoon MCT oil

Directions: Combine ingredients in a small saucepan and heat slightly to a boil. Adjust liquid to desired consistency by adding a little more water or broth. Remove from heat and chill. Enjoy over salad. Makes 2-3 servings (1 vegetable)

Italian Vinaigrette

Ingredients
½ cup low sodium chicken or vegetable broth
1 tablespoon MCT oil
2 tablespoon apple cider vinegar
2 tablespoons lemon juice
1 teaspoon organic Italian herb spice blend
2 tablespoons finely minced onion
½ teaspoon garlic powder
½ teaspoon onion powder

Directions: Combine ingredients in small saucepan. Simmer on low heat for 5 minutes to combine flavors. Remove from heat, chill, and serve as a dressing or use as a marinade. Modifications: Omit the lemon juice and stir in low fat sour cream to make creamy Italian dressing.
Makes 2 or more servings

Ketchup

Ingredients
3 ounces tomato paste
3 tablespoons apple cider vinegar
1 tablespoon lemon juice
¼ teaspoon celery salt
½ teaspoon paprika
¼ teaspoon mustard powder
Pinch of nutmeg and clove
Sea Salt to taste
¼ teaspoon onion powder
¼ teaspoon garlic powder
Stevia or Lakanto to taste

Directions: Dissolve spices in vinegar and lemon juice. Add tomato paste and mix thoroughly. Add additional lemon juice, vinegar or a little water until desired consistency is reached.
Makes 2 or more servings (1 vegetable)

Lemon Pepper Marinade

Ingredients
4 tablespoons lemon juice
3 tablespoons low sodium chicken or vegetable broth
Salt and black pepper to taste
1 teaspoon MCT oil

Directions: Mix ingredients together. Marinate protein for 20 or more minutes.
Makes 1-2 servings

Liquid Amino Marinade

Ingredients
¼ cup apple cider Bragg liquid Aminos
1 tablespoon MCT oil

Directions: Combine liquid aminos and MCT and add to any beef, chicken or fish to marinade over night. Bake, broil or BBQ! Makes multiple servings

Marinara Sauce

Ingredients
4 large tomatoes or as many as you want if you wish to increase the recipe
1 cup low sodium chicken or vegetable broth
1 6 ounce can tomato paste
1 tablespoon dried basil or fresh rolled and chopped basil to taste
2 tablespoons minced onion
2 cloves of garlic crushed and minced
1 teaspoon dried oregano
Sea Salt and pepper to taste

Directions: Chop tomatoes or puree in a food processor for a smoother texture, add spices and heat in a saucepan. Allow to slow cook for 30 minutes to an hour. Allow the liquid to reduce or add additional water to achieve desired consistency. Modifications: Add sautéed celery & onion. Makes 2 or more servings (1 vegetable)

Mustard

Ingredients
2 tablespoons ground mustard powder
1 tablespoon turmeric
1 tablespoon paprika
½ cup apple cider vinegar
¼ cup water
Sea Salt to taste
1 tsp fresh lemon juice
Add 1/2 tsp grated horseradish for spicy

Add stevia to taste for sweet mustard

Directions: Mix ingredients together thoroughly, heat in a saucepan for 2-3 minutes. Pack warm mustard into a jar and top with lemon juice. Mustard will last up to two weeks in the refrigerator. Add water as needed for consistency. FYI: Most mustards are healthy- read your ingredient deck! Makes 1-2 servings

Orange Tarragon Marinade for Chicken or Fish

Ingredients
¼ cup low sodium chicken or vegetable broth
2 tablespoons apple cider vinegar
½ fresh orange juiced
1 clove of garlic crushed and minced
1 teaspoon fresh tarragon chopped
¼ teaspoon onion powder
1 teaspoon MCT oil
Salt and pepper to taste

Directions: Combine liquid ingredients with spices and cook on low heat for 3 minutes. Remove from heat and cool. Marinate chicken or fish for 20 minutes or more. Cook chicken or fish in remaining marinade. Deglaze the pan periodically with a little water. Save the sauce and add apple cider vinegar to make additional dressing for a salad. Serve over a mixed green salad or other vegetable.
Makes 1 serving (1 fruit)

Papa's Pesto Sauce

Ingredients
2 cups Fresh Basil leaves, packed
1/4 cup Fresh Parsley, packed
4 cloves raw garlic, minced
1/3 cup pine nuts
1/4 cup grated Parmesan cheese
1/2 cup MCT Oil or Extra Virgin Olive Oil (depending on diet)
Sea Salt and black pepper to taste

Directions: Combine the basil in with the pine nuts, pulse a few times in a food processor. (If you are using walnuts instead of pine nuts and they are not already chopped, pulse them a few times first, before adding the basil.) Add the garlic, pulse a few times more. Slowly add the MCT/olive oil in a constant stream while the food processor is on. Stop to scrape down the sides of the food processor with a rubber spatula. Add the grated cheese and pulse again until blended. Add a pinch of salt and freshly ground black pepper to taste. Pesto sauce may be added to vegetables or other protein options. Modifications: Use walnuts instead of pine nuts and use Romano Cheese or Parmesan combo.
Makes 8-12 servings of pesto sauce.

Savory Dill Dressing & Marinade

Ingredients
Fresh dill minced
2 tablespoons lemon juice
2 tablespoons apple cider vinegar
2 tablespoon low sodium chicken or vegetable broth
1 tablespoon MCT oil
Salt and pepper to taste

Directions: Combine ingredients and allow the flavors to marinate for 30 minutes or more and serve as a marinade for fish or a dressing for vegetables or salad. For use as a marinade, double or triple the recipe as needed.
Makes 1 serving

Spicy Orange Sauce

Ingredients
½ orange rolled and slightly juiced with rind
½ lemon slightly juiced and with rind
½ cup water
1 tablespoon minced green onion
1 clove crushed garlic
¼ teaspoon ginger powder
¼ teaspoon garlic powder
Pinch of orange and lemon zest
Pinch of cayenne pepper
1tsp Bragg Liquid Amino

Directions: In a small saucepan add slightly juiced orange with rind and ½ lemon with rind to water. Bring to a boil, reduce heat and simmer adding water as needed. Simmer until the pulp comes out of the rinds. Scrape out the pulp and discard the rinds. Continue stirring and reducing down the liquid by half until desired consistency is reached. Add onion, Braggs and spices. Add chicken, white fish or beef and sauté or

pour spicy orange sauce over desired cooked protein. Serve with remaining orange slices for garnish.
Makes 1-2 servings (1 fruit)

Strawberry or Berry Vinaigrette

Ingredients
Strawberries or other berries
1 tablespoon apple cider vinegar
1 tablespoon lemon juice
1 tablespoon MCT oil
Dash of sea salt
Fresh ground black pepper to taste
Stevia or Lakanto to taste

Directions: Combine all ingredients in food processor. Puree until smooth. Pour over fresh green salad. Garnish with sliced strawberries or berries and freshly ground black pepper. Variations: use as a marinade or sauce for chicken.
Makes 1 serving (1 fruit)

Sweet and Spicy Mustard Dressing

Ingredients
2 tablespoons homemade mustard recipe (See recipe)
1/2 tsp grated horseradish
1 tablespoon Bragg's liquid aminos
Pinch of ginger
1 clove garlic finely minced
1 tablespoon minced onion
Stevia or Lakanto to taste
Water to desired consistency

Directions: Dissolve spices in liquid ingredients. Mix thoroughly and heat slightly in a saucepan. Add a little water or extra vinegar to create desired consistency.
Makes 1-2 servings

Sweet Orange Dressing & Marinade

Ingredients
Juice of 3 orange juice segments
2 tablespoons lemon juice
1 teaspoon apple cider vinegar (optional)
¼ teaspoon ginger powder
Pinch of turmeric
Pinch of orange zest
Stevia or Lakanto to taste

Directions: Dissolve spices and stevia in juice mixture. Heat the dressing slightly in a saucepan then chill until ready to use. You may double the recipe for a marinade by adding 1 teaspoon MCT oil. Serve with remaining orange slices.
Makes 1 serving (1 fruit)

Sweet Wasabi Dipping Sauce/Marinade

Ingredients
¼ teaspoon wasabi powder or to taste (Japanese horseradish)
2 or more tablespoons Bragg liquid aminos
1/4 tsp Bragg Nutritional Yeast Seasoning
1 tablespoon lemon juice
1 teaspoon MCT oil
Stevia to taste

Directions: Mix wasabi into Bragg's, MCT oil and add lemon juice and stevia to taste.
Makes 1 serving

Tarragon and Garlic Infusion & Marinade

Ingredients
2-3 sprigs of fresh tarragon
½ cup of apple cider vinegar
2 tablespoons lemon juice
2 cloves of garlic crushed and minced
1 TBS Bragg Liquid Aminos
1 tablespoon diced onion
1 teaspoon salt
1 teaspoon MCT oil
Fresh ground black or white pepper

Directions: Pour vinegar and lemon juice into a lidded jar. Add sprigs of tarragon, garlic, onion, aminos, and spices. Marinate overnight or up to a week. Enjoy with fish, chicken, or as a marinade or dressing.
Makes 1-2 servings

Teriyaki Sauce

Ingredients
½ cup beef or chicken broth (Depending on your protein choice)
¼ cup Bragg's liquid aminos
2 tablespoons apple cider or red wine vinegar
Orange juice (Juice from 3 segments)
¼ cup lemon juice
1 tablespoon finely minced onion
1 teaspoon garlic powder

1 teaspoon onion powder
½ teaspoon powdered ginger or grated fresh ginger
1 clove finely minced garlic
Lemon and/or orange zest to taste
Stevia or Lakanto to taste

Directions: Combine all ingredients in a small saucepan and bring to a boil. Reduce heat and simmer for 20 minutes or until liquid is reduced. The longer you simmer the richer the flavors. As the liquid reduces, deglaze the pan with a little MCT oil or broth to intensify the flavors. Enjoy as a glaze or sauce with chicken or beef.
Makes 1-2 servings (1 fruit)

Tomato Picante Dressing

Ingredients
1 medium tomato chopped
1 8 ounce can tomato sauce
1 clove garlic crushed and chopped
1 teaspoon mustard powder
2 tablespoons lemon or lime juice
½ teaspoon ground cumin
½ teaspoon chili powder
Pinch cayenne pepper
Salt and black pepper to taste
Apple cider vinegar to taste

Directions: Put tomato and garlic into food processor and puree. Add mustard, lemon juice, cumin, chili powder, cayenne, and salt and tomato sauce. Blend until smooth. Transfer to a jar and refrigerate. Stir before using.
Makes 2-4 servings (1 vegetable)

SOUPS

Asparagus Parm Soup

Ingredients
4-5 stalks asparagus
2 cups chicken or vegetable broth (or substitute 1 cup water for 1 cup broth)
3 tablespoons Bragg's liquid aminos
2 tablespoons chopped onion
¼ teaspoon thyme
¼ teaspoon garlic powder
¼ teaspoon onion powder
1 bay leaf
1 tablespoon Romano/parmesan cheese
Salt and pepper to taste

Directions: Trim asparagus to remove the tough ends of the stalk and steam until soft. Puree asparagus with broth and spices in a blender or food processor. Heat soup in a saucepan and enjoy. Add 100 grams diced chicken if desired.
Makes 1 serving (1 vegetable)

Beef & Mushroom Thai Soup

Ingredients
100 grams lean beef
1/2 cup Celery
1/2 cup mushrooms of your choice, chopped
2 cups low sodium beef or vegetable broth
3 tablespoons Bragg's liquid aminos
1 tablespoon chopped green onion
1 clove of garlic crushed and minced
Fresh cilantro
½ teaspoon fresh grated ginger
1/8 teaspoon chili powder or red pepper flakes
1 bay leaf
Pinch of cinnamon
Stevia to taste
Sea Salt and pepper to taste

Directions: Heat up broth. Add dry spices, bay leaf, Bragg's, garlic and onion and bring to a boil. Reduce heat and simmer for 5 minutes. Add beef, mushrooms and celery and cook for 20 to 30 minutes until soft. Add salt, pepper, and stevia. Garnish with fresh chopped cilantro. Modifications: Add a few bean sprouts to the soup.
Makes 1 serving (1 protein, 1 vegetable)

Broccoli Soup

Ingredients
2 cups broccoli
2 cups low sodium vegetable broth
1 tablespoon minced onion
2 cloves garlic crushed and sliced
1 TBS Bragg Liquid Amino
Sea Salt and black pepper to taste

Directions: Puree broccoli with broth and spices in blender or food processor. Heat soup in saucepan, simmer on low heat for 5-10 minutes. Serve hot. Sprinkle with parmesan cheese.
Makes 1 serving (1 vegetable) Modification: Add 1 TBS for Cream of Broccoli soup

Celery Soup

Ingredients
Celery (may use celery from crock pot cooking or 1 baked celery recipe)
2 cups low sodium chicken broth
(or substitute 1 cup water for 1 cup broth)
¼ teaspoon thyme
1 bay leaf
¼ teaspoon dried basil
Salt and pepper to taste

Directions: Cook celery until very soft or use crock-pot or vegetable broth cooked celery. Puree in a food processor or blender with broth and spices. Simmer in a saucepan for 20-30 minutes.
Makes 1 serving (1 vegetable) Modification: add 1 TBS of Romano / Parmesan cheese. Add 1 TBS Half & Half for Cream of Celery Soup.

Chicken Broth

Ingredients
3 large chicken breasts

10 or more cups of water
½ large onion chopped
4 stalks of celery chopped
4 cloves of garlic sliced
1 bay leaf
1+ tsp Bragg Liquid Amino
Sea Salt and pepper to taste

Directions: In a large soup pot or crock pot combine chicken and 10 or more cups of water. Water should slightly cover the chicken. Add celery and spices. Heat to a boil then reduce heat to simmer. Allow to slow cook for 4 hours. Remove vegetables and chicken from broth. Refrigerate stock and skim off the chicken fat. Put through a strainer for a clear broth. Makes multiple servings. Modification: Remove bones & bay leaf from broth add the chicken back into broth along with more celery and any veggies you want! Add 1 TBS Half & Half for Cream of Chicken soup

Chicken Tomato & Cabbage Soup (can substitute beef and beef broth)

Ingredients
100 grams chicken breast cubed
1/4 head sliced Cabbage
1/2 cup fresh chopped tomato
2 cups low sodium chicken broth (or substitute 1 cup water for 1 cup broth)
2 tablespoons Bragg's amino acids (optional)
2 cloves garlic crushed and minced
1 tablespoon chopped onion
¼ teaspoon thyme
¼ teaspoon rosemary
Salt and pepper to taste

Directions: Combine chicken, liquids, herbs and spices in medium saucepan. Bring broth to a boil. Add cabbage. Reduce heat, add tomato and simmer for a minimum of 30 minutes. Add additional water to broth as needed. Variations: change the spices and add fresh tarragon or turmeric. Makes 1 serving (1 protein, 1 vegetable)

Crab Bisque

Ingredients
100 grams crab meat
1 cup tomatoes chopped
2 cups low sodium vegetable broth
(or substitute 1 cup water for 1 cup broth)
1 tablespoon onion minced
1 clove garlic crushed and minced
1 teaspoon Mrs. Dash seasoning

1 bay leaf
1 tablespoon half and half milk
Cayenne pepper to taste
Salt and black pepper to taste

Directions: Puree tomatoes and broth in a food processor or blender. Heat up mixture in a small saucepan. Add the crab and spices and simmer for 20-30 minutes stirring frequently. Makes 1 serving (1 protein, 1 vegetable)

Fennel Soup

Ingredients
Fennel bulbs chopped
2 cups chicken or vegetable broth (or substitute 1 cup water for 1 cup broth)
1 tablespoon finely minced onion
¼ teaspoon allspice seasoning blend
Sea Salt and pepper to taste

Directions: Add chopped fennel bulbs, spices, and minced onion to vegetable broth. Heat in small saucepan and simmer for 20 minutes. Add lemon with rind to the broth if desired. Serve warm with chopped sprigs of fennel for garnish.
Makes 1 serving (1 vegetable)

Hot and Sour Chicken or Shrimp Soup

Ingredients
100 grams chicken breast diced
1 cup low sodium chicken or vegetable broth
1 cup water
4 tablespoons apple cider vinegar
4 tablespoons Bragg's liquid aminos
½ lemon in quarters with rind
1 clove garlic crushed and minced
2 tablespoons minced onion
Cayenne pepper to taste
Pinch of chili powder or red chili flakes
Sea Salt and pepper to taste
Stevia or Lakanto to taste (optional)

Directions: Boil lemon wedges with rind in 1 cup of water until pulp comes out of the rind. Scrape out additional pulp and juice. Add the diced chicken or shrimp, spices and chicken or vegetable broth. Simmer until cooked. Variation: You can add orange juice or substitute shrimp for chicken. Makes 1 serving (1 protein) Modifications: Add vegetables such as zucchini or mushrooms.

Minestrone Chicken Soup

Ingredients
200 grams boneless chicken breast (2 chicken breasts), small cubes
1- 32oz low sodium chicken broth
1- 15oz can low sodium Italian Stewed Tomatoes
1- 8oz bag of chopped frozen spinach
1/2 cup onion, chopped
1/2 cup celery, chopped
1 small zucchini, chopped
1/2 cup lentils, washed/cooked
2 cloves garlic crushed and minced
1 TBS Bragg Liquid amino
2 tsp Italian seasoning
Sea Salt and pepper to taste

Directions: Bring all ingredients to boil in medium sauce pan, simmer for 20-30 minutes, add cooked lentils in last 5 minutes. Serve and enjoy.
Modification/Maintenance: Add 1 can red kidney beans or black beans (drained & wash in cold water) instead of lentils for a variety.
Makes 2+ servings (1 protein, 1 vegetable, 1 legume)

Mushroom Soup

Ingredients
2 cups mushrooms of your choice, chopped
2 cups low sodium vegetable broth
1/2 cup white or yellow onion
1 TBS Bragg Liquid Amino
1 TBS MCT
1 tsp Butter Buds
1 tsp thyme, minced
Sea salt & pepper to taste

Directions: Put MCT & Butter Buds in medium sauce pan and sauté mushrooms & onions until lightly golden. Add vegetable broth and spices, simmer 5 minutes. Serve hot. Makes one serving (1 fruit) Modifications: Add 1 TBS half and half for Cream of Mushroom Soup.

Quick Chicken Vegetable Soup

Ingredients
200 grams chicken breast, small cubes
1- 32oz low sodium vegetable or chicken broth
1/2 cup sweet or white onion
4 stalks celery, chopped

4 asparagus spears, chopped
1 cup broccoli, chopped
1 TBS Bragg Liquid Amino
Sea Salt and pepper to taste

Directions: Bring all the ingredients to a boil in medium sauce pan. Simmer for 10-15 minutes, until chicken and vegetables are done. Makes 2 Servings

Shrimp &/or Chicken Gumbo

Ingredients
100 grams shrimp and/or chicken/turkey sausage
2 cups low sodium vegetable broth
1 large tomato chopped
3 tablespoons tomato paste
2 tablespoons white onion
2 cloves of garlic crushed and minced
3 tablespoons apple cider vinegar
Dash of Bragg liquid amino's to taste
Cayenne pepper to taste
MCT oil (for frying)
Sea Salt and pepper to taste

Directions: Sauté shrimp or chicken sausage in a skillet with onions. Add tomato paste, tomatoes, and broth. Mix well. Add the spices and vinegar. Simmer for 20-30 minutes. Serve hot and garnish with fresh parsley. Modification: Mix protein ingredients like shrimp, crab, chicken & chicken sausage. Add additional vegetables such as celery, and bell pepper. Makes 1 serving (1 protein, 1 vegetable)

Tomato Soup

Ingredients
2 cups low sodium chicken or vegetable broth
2 cups chopped fresh tomatoes
3 ounces of tomato paste
2 TBS chopped onion
1 clove garlic crushed & minced
1 TBS Half & Half (if applicable)
1 teaspoon garlic powder
¼ teaspoon dried oregano
Pinch of marjoram
Sea Salt and black pepper to taste

Directions: Puree all ingredients in a food processor or blender. Pour into a saucepan and heat to a boil. Reduce heat and simmer for 20 to 30 minutes. Serve hot, garnish with fresh basil leaves or parsley. Makes 2 servings (1 vegetable)

Turkey Chili

Ingredients
1 lb ground Turkey Breast
1- 16oz can chopped tomatoes (low sodium)
1- 8oz can low sodium tomato sauce
1 small onion or 1/2 medium, chopped
4 stalks of celery, chopped
1 clove garlic crushed and minced
1/2 tsp dried parsley flakes
1/2 tsp dried basil, crushed
¼ cup dry red wine (optional)
1/2 tsp dried oregano, crushed
1/4 tsp ground red pepper
1/4 tsp ground cinnamon
1 TBS chili powder (more if you like it hot)
1 bay leaf
Sea Salt and pepper to taste

Directions: Brown turkey in large skillet until no longer pink, drain off any fat. Stir in undrained tomatoes, (drained kidney beans if applicable), tomato sauce, onion, wine (if desired) and spices. Simmer uncovered for 45 minutes, stirring occasionally. Modification: Replace turkey with leanest ground beef. Makes 4+ servings (1 protein, 1 vegetable,) Maintenance: Add 1- 15oz can red kidney beans, drain & rinse in cold water. (1 legume) Dana's Favorite!

Vegetable Beef Soup

Ingredients
100 grams lean beef cubed
1/2 cup Celery
1/2 cup cabbage
1 small tomato, diced
2 cups low sodium beef or vegetable broth
1 tablespoon onion chopped
1 clove garlic crushed and minced
1 bay leaf
1/8 teaspoon dried basil
1/8 teaspoon fresh or dried oregano
Pinch of thyme
Pinch of paprika
Pinch of chili powder
Sea Salt and pepper to taste

Directions: Combine onion, garlic and spices with beef broth. Add celery, cabbage and diced beef. Simmer for 20-30 minutes. Add tomatoes and simmer for an additional 5

minutes.
Makes 1 serving (1 protein, 1 vegetable) Modifications: Add additional vegetables such as zucchini, bell peppers. Maintenance: add barley

Vegetable Broth

Ingredients
10 or more cups of water
½ large onion chopped
6-10 stalks celery
8 cloves of garlic chopped
2 bay leaves
1 teaspoon paprika
1 teaspoon garlic powder
1 teaspoon basil
1 teaspoon of thyme
1+ tsp Bragg Liquid Amino
Salt and pepper to taste

Directions: Bring water to a boil in a large soup pot or crock-pot. Add vegetables and spices. Slow cook for 2-4 hours. Strain out vegetables and cool. Use as a base for soups.
Makes multiple servings

Vegetable Ginger Soup

Ingredients
2 cups low sodium vegetable broth (or substitute 1 cup water for 1 cup broth)
2 Tomatoes chopped, 8 ounces tomato sauce or 3 ounces tomato paste
2 celery stalks, chopped
1 clove garlic crushed and minced
1 tablespoon onion chopped
1/8 teaspoon ginger
¼ teaspoon cumin
Salt and black pepper to taste
Fresh parsley, cilantro or mint

Directions: Combine broth, tomato sauce, and celery. Bring to a boil. Reduce heat and add spices. Simmer for 20-30 minutes or until vegetables are tender.
Makes 1 serving (1 vegetable)
Modifications: Add zucchini or other veggies of your choice

POULTRY ENTREES

Asian Ginger Chicken

Ingredients
100 grams chicken breast (beat it)
¼ cup low sodium chicken broth or water
4 tablespoons lemon juice
¼ teaspoon lemon or orange zest
½ teaspoon fresh ginger
4 tablespoons Bragg's liquid aminos
1 tablespoon chopped onion
MCT oil (for sauté)
Salt and pepper to taste
Cayenne pepper to taste

Directions: In a fry pan, sauté chicken in a little lemon juice and water until slightly browned. Add spices, ginger, salt, lemon and stevia. Add Bragg's liquid aminos and cook thoroughly. Deglaze the pan periodically by adding a little water. Serve hot and garnish with lemon or orange slices. Makes 1 serving (1 protein)

Baked Apple Chicken

Ingredients
100 grams cubed chicken
½ finely chopped apple
2 tablespoons lemon juice
1 tablespoon apple cider vinegar
1/8 teaspoon cinnamon
Sea Salt and pepper to taste
MCT oil (for browning chicken)
Dash of cayenne

Directions: Lightly brown the chicken in lemon juice. Add chopped apple and evenly coat with a mixture of apple cider vinegar, lemon juice, stevia, cinnamon, cayenne and pinch of salt. Put in small baking dish and add additional vinegar and lemon juice. Serve with the rest of the apple in thin slices on the side.
Makes 1 serving (1 protein, 1 fruit)

Barbecued Chicken

Ingredients
100 grams of chicken breast whole
1 serving of barbecue sauce (see recipe)
Spray MCT oil

Directions: Coat chicken with barbeque sauce and fry, bake or grill coat with MCT oil until cooked thoroughly on low heat. Watch closely so that it doesn't burn on grill/barbeque. Serve hot. Add salt and pepper to taste.
Makes 1 serving (1 protein, 1 vegetable)

Chicken Cacciatore

Ingredients
100 grams diced chicken breast
1-2 cups chopped tomatoes
¼ cup low sodium chicken broth
2 tablespoons tomato paste
1 tablespoon apple cider vinegar
2 tablespoons lemon juice
1 tablespoon Bragg's liquid aminos
2 tablespoons chopped onion
2 TBS celery, chopped
2 cloves crushed and minced garlic
¼ tsp onion powder
¼ tsp garlic powder
1/2 tsp Bragg Natural Yeast Seasoning
1 bay leaf
MCT oil (browning chicken)

Directions: Brown the chicken with garlic, onion, celery and lemon juice in a small saucepan. Deglaze the pan with the chicken broth. Add tomatoes, tomato paste, vinegar and spices. Simmer on low heat for 20 minutes stirring occasionally. Remove the bay leaf and serve hot.
Makes 1 serving (1 protein, 1 vegetable) Modification: Serve over Miracle Noodles

Chicken Curry

Ingredients
100 grams cubed chicken
¼ cup low sodium chicken broth
¼ teaspoon curry powder or to taste
Pinch of turmeric
Dash of garlic powder
Dash of onion powder
1 tablespoon minced onion
1 tsp Bragg liquid amino
Sea Salt and pepper to taste
MCT oil (for sauté)
Cayenne to taste

Directions: Dissolve spices and Bragg's in chicken broth in a small saucepan. Add chopped onion, garlic and chicken. Add Stevia to taste for a more sweet curry. Sauté chicken in liquid until fully cooked and liquid is reduced by half. Additional water may be added to achieve desired consistency. Serve hot or cold. Makes 1 serving (1 protein)

Chicken Paprika

Ingredients
100 grams chicken breast, (beat it)
½ cup low sodium chicken broth
3 tablespoons tomato paste
1 teaspoon paprika
1/4 tsp cumin
1 tablespoon chopped red onion
1 clove garlic crushed and minced
1+ tsp Braggs Liquid Amino's
1 bay leaf
Sea Salt and pepper to taste

Directions: Combine broth, chicken, Braggs, garlic, and onion. Stir in tomato paste and spices. Simmer chicken mixture for 20 minutes or more. Serve with sliced tomatoes or veggie of your choice! Makes 1 serving (1 protein, 1 vegetable) Modifications: Sauté the chicken in MCT oil and Butter Buds, then add tomato and broth.

Chicken Pesto

Ingredients
100 grams chicken breast, cubed
2 cloves of garlic, sliced
1 TBS MCT Oil
Sea Salt and pepper to taste
Papa's Pesto (see recipe)

Directions: Fry chicken in MCT oil, garlic, salt and pepper in a pan until lightly browned and cooked thoroughly. Add pesto mixture to chicken, add a little water and cook on medium heat coating chicken with pesto mixture. Serve hot over Miracle Noodles Orzo. Pesto sauce may be made by itself and added to vegetables or other protein options. Makes 1 serving (1 protein) Makes 2-3 servings of pesto sauce.

Chicken & Spinach Rolls

Ingredients
100 grams chicken breast (beat it)
2 cups Spinach
½ cup low sodium chicken broth
1 tablespoon chopped onion

1 clove of garlic crushed and minced
1 tablespoon lemon juice
Dash of onion powder
Dash of garlic powder
Dash of cumin
Mrs. Dash Garlic & Herb to taste
Sea Salt and pepper to taste

Directions: Tenderize chicken manually by pounding until flat. Cook spinach lightly with garlic, onion and spices. Strain out excess liquid from the spinach and place mound of spinach in the center of the pounded chicken. Roll up the spinach mixture inside the chicken breast. Place rolls in baking dish and add
chicken broth to the pan. Bake the rolls in 350 degree oven for about 15-20 minutes or until chicken is cooked completely. Modifications: Top with marinara sauce recipe bake until brown and bubbly. Makes 1 serving (1 protein, 1 vegetable)

Chicken Tacos &/or Taco Salad

Ingredients
Taco Meat filling:
1lb finely chopped or ground chicken breast, Turkey breast or leanest ground beef
1 cup low sodium chicken or beef broth
1 tablespoon chopped onion
2 cloves garlic crushed and minced
1/8 teaspoon dried oregano
1/8 crushed red pepper to flakes
1/2 tsp ground cumin
1 tsp chili powder to taste
1/4 tsp ground paprika
1/4 tsp Sea Salt
1/4 tsp black pepper
1 tsp Braggs Liquid Aminos
MCT Oil (for browning)
Taco Condiments:
2-4 large lettuce leaves
1 tomato chopped
1/2 cup onion, chopped

Directions: Spray MCT in frying pan. Cook/brown chicken, turkey or beef. Add onion, garlic, spices to broth in measuring cup, then pour over meat, simmer 5-10 minutes. Serve meat filling, taco style in butter lettuce or romaine leaf wrap. Or make a big salad & top with veggies or salsa (See recipe) Makes 4 servings (1 protein, 1 vegetable) Maintenance: Serve with low-carb whole grain tortilla, black olives, avocado, shredded Mozzarella cheese, black beans, Miracle Noodle Rice, etc

Chicken Tarragon

Ingredients
100 grams chicken breast
¼ cup tarragon and garlic infusion (see recipe)
¼ cup chicken broth or water
2 tablespoons lemon juice
½ teaspoon fresh chopped tarragon
1 tablespoon chopped onion
1 clove garlic minced
Dash of mustard powder
MCT oil (for sauté)

Directions: Heat the chicken broth, vinegar, garlic, and onion in a small saucepan or frying pan. Add chicken and sauté for about 10 minutes or until chicken is completely cooked and liquid is reduced. Deglaze the pan periodically with a little water to create a sauce. Serve hot. Makes 1 serving (1 protein)

Chunky Crock Pot Chicken

Ingredients
1 lb boneless chicken breast, cubed
½ cup chopped onion
1 cup celery, sliced
1 cup mushroom slices
2 cups low sodium chicken broth
2 cups water
4 cloves fresh chopped garlic
Try 1 TBS *Real Salt Natural Seasoning*
OR 3/4 teaspoon paprika
1 tsp sea salt
½ tsp coriander
1 teaspoon onion powder
1/2 tsp black pepper
1 teaspoon garlic powder

Directions: Put all the ingredients in crock-pot and cover. Cook low for 6 hours or high for 3 hrs. Modifications/Maintenance: add carrots, red potatoes, 3/4 cup pearl barley or packages of frozen vegetables for soup or stew. Makes about 3 quarts. Double recipe for 5 qts. Makes 1 serving (1 protein, 1 vegetable)

Dana's Turkey Sausage Goulash

Ingredients
1lb ground turkey sausage
1/2 cup white onion
1/2 cup celery

1- 14.5 can low sodium stewed tomatoes
1- 14.5 can low sodium tomato sauce
1 tsp Italian seasoning
3 cloves diced garlic
Sea Salt and pepper to taste

Directions: Brown sausage and cook thoroughly. Add canned undrained stewed tomatoes & sauce, onion, celery, seasonings, garlic, salt and pepper. Simmer for 10 minutes. Modifications: Add black olives, carrots and spoon over whole grain pasta or Miracle Noodles. Makes 1 serving (1 protein, 1 vegetable)

Lemon Chicken

Ingredients
100 grams thinly sliced chicken
½ lemon with rind
1 tablespoon Bragg's liquid aminos
¼ cup low sodium chicken broth or water
1 cup water
Mrs. Dash Lemon Pepper to taste
Sea Salt to taste
Stevia to taste (for Sweet Lemon Chicken)

Directions: Slice up ½ lemons in to quarters and add to water. In a small saucepan boil lemon quarters until pulp comes out of the rind. Add broth, chicken, Bragg's and spices and simmer on low heat until chicken is cooked and sauce is reduced by half. Deglaze periodically with water if necessary. Garnish with fresh lemon slices, lemon zest or mint. Makes 1 serving (1 protein)

Middle Eastern Spicy Chicken

Ingredients
100 grams chicken breast, cubed
1 cup chopped fresh tomatoes
½ cup low sodium chicken broth or water
3 tablespoons lemon juice
1 tablespoon minced onion
1 clove garlic crushed and minced
1/8 teaspoon fresh grated ginger
¼ teaspoon allspice
Dash of cumin
Dash of cinnamon
Mrs. Dash Caribbean Citrus to taste
Sea Salt and black pepper to taste

Directions: Combine spices with liquid ingredients. Bring to a boil. Add tomatoes and

chicken to the sauce. Simmer for 20-30 minutes and serve.
Makes 1 serving (1 protein 1 vegetable)

Moroccan Lemon Chicken

Ingredients
100 grams chicken breast (beat it)
Juice of ½ lemon
1 tablespoon minced onion
Pinch of ginger
Pinch of ground coriander
Pinch of saffron
Pinch of lemon zest
MCT oil
Lemon slices
Mrs. Dash Lemon Pepper to taste

Directions: Marinate saffron strands in lemon juice then crush into a paste. Add dry spices. Dip chicken breast in lemon juice and spice mixture. Rub oil & additional spices into chicken breast with salt and pepper. Wrap individual servings in foil and cover with slices of lemon and a little of the saffron mixture. Bake chicken at 350 for 20-30 minutes or until chicken is cooked completely and tender. Makes 1 serving (1 protein)

Mustard Chicken

Ingredients
100 grams chicken breast (beat it)
½ cup low sodium chicken broth or water
2 tablespoons lemon juice
1 tablespoon homemade mustard (see recipe)
¼ teaspoon dried basil
1/8 teaspoon tarragon
Salt and pepper to taste
MCT oil (sauté chicken)

Directions: Lightly sauté the chicken in chicken broth, lemon juice, and spices until cooked. Simmer for additional 10 minutes and periodically deglaze the pan with a little water or additional broth to make the sauce. Makes 1 serving (1 protein) Modifications: Use sweet or spicy mustard if desired. Try Mrs. Dash Extra Spicy or stevia for sweet mustard chicken.

Orange Chicken

Ingredients
100 grams chicken breast (beat it)
Choose Sweet or Spicy

One serving spicy orange sauce or sweet orange marinade (see recipes)

Directions: Prepare orange sauce. Beat then cook chicken with the sauce in pan with the juices or bake in oven at 375 degrees for approximately 20-30 minutes or until cooked thoroughly. In a saucepan reduce liquid until desired consistency. Deglaze the pan periodically by adding water and pour remaining mixture over chicken breast.
Modifications: Serve with Miracle Noodle Rice & sautéed snow peas.
Makes 1 serving (1 protein, 1 fruit)

Spanish Style Green Chili Chicken

Ingredients
100 grams cubed or sliced chicken
1 cup Chopped tomatoes
½ cup low sodium chicken broth or water
2 tablespoons lemon juice
1 small can mild green chili's
1/4 cup chopped onion
¼ teaspoon dried oregano
¼ clove fresh garlic minced
¼ teaspoon chili powder
Cayenne or ground red pepper to taste
Pinch of cumin
Mrs. Dash Fiesta line to taste
Salt and pepper to taste

Directions: Lightly brown the chicken with a little lemon juice. Add spices, additional lemon juice, and chicken broth. When the chicken is cooked thoroughly, add fresh tomatoes, chili's and cook for 5-10 more minutes or throw it all in a crockpot!
Modification: Use medium or hot chili's if you like it hot! Put over Miracle Noodle Rice!
Makes 1 serving (1 protein 1 vegetable)

Sweet and Sour Chicken

Ingredients
100 grams chicken breast
½ orange, ½ lemon with rind
1 cup water
1 tablespoon Bragg's liquid aminos
2 tablespoons apple cider vinegar
1 tablespoon minced onion
1 tablespoon lemon and/or orange zest
Dash of garlic powder
Dash of onion powder
1 ground red pepper
Cayenne pepper to taste

Salt and pepper to taste
Stevia or Lakanto to taste

Directions: In a frying pan or small saucepan place ½ orange and ½ lemons with the rind in water and boil until pulp comes out of the rind. Remove rinds from the water and scrap out remaining pulp and juice with a spoon. Add spices, onion, and stevia to taste. Add chicken and cook until liquid is reduced by approximately half and desired consistency is achieved. Add onion and garlic powders which act as slight thickening agent. Serve hot and garnish with lemon. Makes 1 serving (1 protein, 1 fruit)
Modifications: Add a small amount bell pepper and chopped mushrooms.

Szechwan Chicken & Cabbage

Ingredients
100 grams chicken breast (beat it)
2 cups shredded green Cabbage
1 cup low sodium chicken broth or water
3 tablespoons Bragg's liquid aminos
1 teaspoon red pepper
Pinch of crushed red pepper flakes
Pinch of fresh or powdered ginger
1 clove garlic crushed and minced
1 tablespoon chopped green onion
Stevia or Lakanto to taste

Directions: Brown Chicken in Bragg's and a little water. Add chicken broth and spices. Simmer for 5 minutes. Add the cabbage and allow to cook for 10 minutes or until cabbage is tender. Add additional water if necessary. Top with additional green onions for garnish and sprinkle with lemon juice and additional Bragg's.
Makes 1 serving (1 protein, 1 vegetable)

Teriyaki Turkey Burgers

Ingredients
1 lb ground turkey or chicken breast
1/2 cup sweet onion, diced small

2 tablespoons Bragg's liquid aminos
Sea Salt and pepper to taste
MCT oil for browning

Directions: Mix turkey, onion and Braggs in bowl. Make 4 patties, BBQ or fry with MCT & sea salt in pan and cook on medium heat for about 5-10 minutes or until turkey is thoroughly cooked, brown on each side. Periodically deglaze the pan with a little water to create a richer flavor or put the cover on after both sides are brown to get moisture and flavor.
Makes 4 servings (1 protein)

Tomato Basil Chicken

Ingredients
100 grams cubed chicken breast
1 cup chopped tomato
¼ cup low sodium chicken broth or water
2 tablespoons lemon juice
2 tablespoons chopped onion
1-2 cloves garlic sliced
3 leaves basil rolled and sliced
1/8 teaspoon oregano fresh or dried
Mrs. Dash Tomato Basil Garlic
Dash of garlic powder
Dash of onion powder
MCT oil (browning chicken)
Salt and pepper to taste

Directions: Lightly brown the chicken in small saucepan with lemon juice. Add garlic, onion, spices and water. After chicken is cooked add fresh tomatoes and basil. Continue cooking for 5-10 minutes. Salt and pepper to taste, garnish with fresh basil.
Makes 1 serving (1 protein, 1 vegetable)

Turkey Sausages & Patties

Ingredients
1 lb turkey sausage patties or links
MCT oil (for browning)

Directions: Easy!! Purchase Turkey Store or Foster Farms Turkey Sausage links or patties. Cook thoroughly until lightly browned. Eat for breakfast with eggs or cut up/ ground up in sauces and stir frys for a different taste!
Makes 6 servings (1 protein)

BEEF ENTREES

Beef Bourguignon

Ingredients
100 grams lean beef cubed
1 cup low sodium beef broth or water
3 tablespoons tomato paste
4 pearl onions, fresh or frozen
1 clove garlic crushed and sliced
1 tsp Bragg Liquid Aminos
1 tsp dried thyme
1 bay leaf
1 whole clove
Sea Salt & pepper to taste

Directions: Lightly braise beef cubes with onion and garlic. Combine all ingredients in small saucepan. Add liquid ingredients and spices. Slow cook for a minimum of 30 minutes or until beef is tender. Add additional water as needed to achieve desired consistency. Makes 1 serving (1 protein, 1 vegetable)
Modifications: Add 1/4 cup mushrooms

Beef or Chicken Fajitas

Ingredients
1 lb sliced lean beef or chicken breast cut into strips
1 medium tomato, chopped
1 small onion, sliced
1 clove garlic minced
1 TBS Bragg Liquid Aminos
1 TBS Apple Cider Vinegar (ACV)
1 green bell pepper, sliced
1 teaspoon chili powder or to taste
Pinch of cayenne pepper
MCT oil (for frying)
1/2 lemon, juiced

Directions: Combine garlic, Braggs, ACV, & spices in medium bowl and marinate meat for 30 minutes at room temperature or cover and refrigerate for several hours. Heat MCT oil in a large skillet over high heat. Add chicken or beef strips to the pan, and sauté for 5 minutes. Add the onion, tomatoes and green pepper, and sauté another 3 minutes. Remove from heat, and sprinkle with lemon juice and tomatoes. Enjoy with lettuce leaf mock tortillas wrap and salsa. Makes 4 servings (1 protein, 1 vegetable)
Modifications: Add multi-colored bell peppers to fajitas.

Beef Kabobs

Ingredients
1 lb of lean beef tip or round OR chicken, cut into 1 1/4 inch cubes
8 small onions
1 large green bell pepper, cut into squares
8 cherry tomatoes
2 cloves garlic, minced
1 cup low sodium beef, chicken, or vegetable broth
3 tablespoons apple cider vinegar
1 tablespoon Bragg's liquid aminos
1/4 tsp onion powder
Sea Salt & Pepper to taste

Directions: Marinate beef or chicken in broth, vinegar, Braggs, garlic and spices for at least 3 hours covered in refrigerator, spooning mixture over kabob occasionally. Layer meat, onions, tomatoes and green pepper on wooden or metal skewers (If using wooden skewers soak them for a few minutes so they don't burn). Barbeque directly or place on aluminum foil sheet and cook until desired level of doneness. Baste frequently with remaining marinade. Heat the remaining marinade in a small sauce pan and use as a dipping sauce. Makes 4 servings (1 protein, 1 fruit)

Beef Stew

Ingredients
1lb lean beef (round, or any other lean steak),
cut in 1 inch cubes
1 medium stalk celery, cut 1 inch pieces
1 medium turnip, cut in 1 inch pieces
1 medium green bell pepper, cut 1 inch pieces
3 cups low sodium beef broth or water
1 small onion, chopped
1 clove garlic crushed and minced
1/8 teaspoon onion powder
1/8 teaspoon garlic powder
1 TBS Bragg Liquid Aminos
1/2 tsp Sea Salt
1/8 tsp pepper
MCT oil (for browning)

Directions: In saucepan, lightly brown cubed beef with MCT oil and garlic. Add broth/water, vegetables, Braggs and spices and bring to a boil. Reduce heat and simmer for approximately 30 minutes to an hour or until the beef is tender. Add water as needed to create a stew like consistency. Serve hot and enjoy. Garnish with parsley. This also works as a crock pot recipe. Just add additional water and slow cook whole 100 gram servings instead of cubed. Makes multiple servings (1 protein, 1 vegetable)

Beef Teriyaki

Ingredients
100 grams sliced boneless beef top loin or sirloin steak*
1 TBS Bragg Liquid Aminos
1/8 tsp ground ginger
1 clove garlic crushed
1 TBS MCT oil
Sea Salt and pepper to taste
Stevia for sweetness to taste

Directions: Trim fat and bone from beef steak; cut beef across grain into 1/8 inch slices. Mix Braggs, oil, ginger and garlic. Stir in beef, coating each slice thoroughly. Cover and refrigerate 1 hr. Drain beef, reserving marinade. Cook and stir beef in skillet over medium heat, stirring frequently, until beef is light brown, about 5 minutes. Add enough cold water to marinade to make 1/4 cup, stir gradually into beef. Heat to boiling, stirring constantly, reduce heat. Simmer uncovered 5 minutes * Beef is easier to slice if partially frozen. Serve with *Miracle Noodle* Rice.
Makes 1 serving (1 protein)

Corned Beef Hash

Ingredients
2 cups left over corned beef (lean only) from corned beef and cabbage recipe
Leftover cabbage
1/2 cup chopped onion
1 TBS parsley, snipped
Pinch of fresh thyme
Pinch of fresh chopped oregano
1/2 tsp Sea Salt
1/8 tsp pepper
MCT oil (for frying)

Directions: Chop up corned beef into finely diced chunks. Combine with finely chopped leftover cabbage and spices and mix well. Preheat non-stick or cast iron skillet. Press corned beef mixture into pan firmly and cover. Cook for approximately 5-6 minutes on medium heat until lightly browned. Add a little beef broth or water to deglaze, mix and press down again cooking for an additional 5-6 minutes. Repeat as necessary until hot and lightly browned. Or bake in greased (spray MCT oil) square baking dish 8x8x2 inches. Cook uncovered in 350 oven for 20 minutes.
Makes 2 servings (1 protein, 1 vegetable)

Corned Beef & Cabbage

Ingredients
2 lb well-trimmed corned beef boneless brisket or round
1 small head green cabbage, cut into 6 wedges
1 small onion cut into fourths
1 clove garlic, crushed
1 teaspoon fresh thyme
1 bay leaf
Bragg Liquid Aminos to taste
Sea Salt and pepper to taste

Directions: Salt and pepper the beef and put meat, onion, garlic and spices into a crock-pot or large pot and add enough cold water to cover. Bring to a boil and then reduce heat, cover and simmer until beef is tender, about 2 hours. Skim the fat from the broth as it rises. Add the cabbage to the pot, heat to boiling; reduce heat, simmer uncovered 15 minutes, or until the meat and cabbage are tender. Slice thinly across the grain and serve with horseradish sauce (see recipe).
Makes 6-8 Servings (1 protein, 1 vegetable)

Ground Beef, Chicken or Turkey Tacos

Ingredients
1 lb lean ground beef, chicken or turkey breast
1 tablespoon finely minced onion
1 clove crushed and minced garlic
1/2 tsp of garlic powder
1/2 tsp of onion powder
1/4 tsp of dried oregano
Fresh chopped cilantro to taste
Cayenne or chili pepper to taste
Sea Salt to taste
Lettuce Leaves
Tomato
MCT oil (for browning)

Directions: Brown ground beef, chicken or turkey. Add onion, garlic, and spices and 1

cup water and simmer gently for 5-10 minutes. Add salt to taste. Serve taco style in butter lettuce or romaine leaf mock tortilla wraps or with a side of tomatoes or salsa. Modifications: Add avocado. Try MRS Dash: Extra Spicy, Southwest Chipotle or Fiesta Lime.
Makes 4 servings (1 protein, 1 vegetable)

Hamburgers

Ingredients
100 grams leanest ground hamburger (less than 7% fat)
1 tablespoon finely minced onion
1 clove finely minced garlic
Dash of garlic powder
Dash of onion powder
Dash Mrs. Dash Hamburger Blend
MCT oil (for frying)

Directions: Mix ingredients thoroughly and form into patty. Fry in small frying pan until desired level of doneness or grill on the barbeque. If using frying pan add small amounts of water and deglaze pan to intensify flavors. Cook approximately 3 minutes each side or to desired level of doneness. Variations: Add Bragg's liquid aminos to create a slight teriyaki flavor or top with caramelized onion. Modifications: Also try lean buffalo or bison meat.
Makes 1 serving (1 protein)

Herbed Crock Pot Roast

Ingredients
1 4lb shoulder roast
4 medium white turnips, cut each into fourths
2 medium stalks celery, cut into 1 inch pieces
1 medium green pepper, cut into 1 inch pieces
2 cloves garlic, crushed
8 small onions
1 cup apple cider vinegar (ACV)
1 tsp dried marjoram leaves
1 TBS Sea Salt
1 tsp black pepper

Directions: Sear roast on high heat with MCT oil on all sides to brown. Place in crock pot. Sprinkle with garlic, marjoram, salt and pepper. Add ACV, turnips, celery, green pepper & onions. Heat on high for 30 minutes then reduce heat to low and cook for 6-8 hrs until fork tender. Save the juice to make sauces and dressings. Skim off any excess fat. Makes multiple servings (1 protein, 1 vegetable)

Italian Beef & Veggie Rolls

Ingredients
100 grams lean flank steak
Finely chopped cabbage or spinach
1 cup low sodium beef broth or water
2 tablespoons apple cider vinegar
2 tablespoons Bragg's liquid aminos
1 clove garlic crushed and minced
1 tablespoon minced onion
1 teaspoon Mrs. Dash Italian Medley
Sea Salt and pepper to taste
MCT oil (for frying)

Directions: Tenderize steak with manual meat tenderizer until flat and thin. In a frying pan combine cabbage or spinach with spices, vinegar and aminos and cook until slightly tender. Spoon cabbage or spinach mixture into pounded flank steak and wrap into a roll. Fill the bottom of the pan with a little water and beef broth. Salt and spice the top of the roll Bake in 375 degree oven for approximately 20 minutes until cooked. Baste occasionally with juices to keep the rolls moist.
Makes 1 serving (1 protein, 1 vegetable)

Italian Meatballs

Ingredients
1 lb leanest ground beef, chicken or turkey breast
1 egg white
2 pieces melba toast, crumbled
2 tablespoons finely minced onion
1 clove of garlic crushed and minced
1 teaspoon basil
1 teaspoon oregano
1 teaspoon onion powder
1 teaspoon garlic powder
1 tsp Sea Salt
1 tsp Bragg liquid aminos
MCT oil (for cooking)

Directions: Mix ingredients; shape into twenty 1 1/2 inch balls. Cook over medium heat, turning occasionally, until brown about 20 minutes. Or cook in ungreased oblong pan, 13x9x2 inches in 400 oven until light brown, 20-25 minutes. Serve with marinara recipe. Or put in crock pot with Marinara sauce on high for 3hrs or low for 6hrs.
Makes 4 servings (1 protein, 1 vegetable)

London Broil Strips

Ingredients
1lb high quality beef flank steak cut into strips*
¼ cup low sodium beef broth or water
1 small onion, thinly sliced
2 cloves garlic, crushed and minced
1/8 teaspoon thyme
1/8 tsp rosemary
1/4 tsp Sea Salt
1/4 tsp pepper
MCT oil (for frying)

Directions: Salt and pepper the beef strips. In a frying pan or non-stick skillet combine beef, herbs and beef broth. Cook until desired level of doneness. *Cut across grain for most tender. Variations: Steak Salad.
Makes 4 servings (1 protein)

Meatloaf

Ingredients
1 lb ground lean ground beef, chicken or turkey breast
1/4 cup celery
1/4 cup onion
1 egg white
1/2 tsp dry mustard
1 TBS Bragg liquid aminos
1/4 tsp ground sage

2 pieces Melba toast, crumbled
1 clove garlic, crushed
1 tsp Sea Salt
1/4 tsp ground black pepper

Directions: Mix all ingredients. Spread in ungreased loaf pan, 9x5x3 inches. Cook uncovered in 350 oven until done, about 1 1/2 hours. Modifications: top with ketchup (see recipe) cover with foil and bake. Check at 1 to 1 1/4 hrs.
Makes 4 servings (1 protein, 1 vegetable)

Minute Steak

Ingredients
1 beef cubed steak (about 3-4 oz)
1 tsp Bragg's liquid aminos
Sea Salt and pepper to taste
1 TBS green onions, chopped
MCT oil (for sauté)

Directions: Coat beef steak with Braggs, salt & pepper. Cook steak in MCT oil over medium-high heat until brown, about 4 minutes on each side. Garnish with the chopped green onions and serve hot.
Makes 1 serving (1 protein)

Pepper Steak

Ingredients
100 grams lean beef sirloin steak
Fresh ground black pepper
1 tsp Bragg liquid aminos
Sea Salt to taste

Directions: Manually tenderize the meat until flat. Rub meat with salt and coat liberally with black pepper. Cook on high heat for about 3-5 minutes or throw on the barbeque.

Top with Braggs if desired and caramelized onions. You can also cut the steak into strips and serve over a mixed green salad.
Makes 1 serving (1 protein)

Sloppy Joes

Ingredients
1 lb leanest ground beef
1/2 cup onion, chopped
1/3 cup celery, chopped
1 recipe barbeque sauce (see recipe)
Butter lettuce or any large variety lettuce leaves
MCT oil (for frying)

Directions: Brown ground beef in small frying pan with onion. Add barbeque sauce, celery and a little water to achieve desired consistency. Cook for about 5 minutes. Serve sloppy Joe style on lettuce leaves.
Makes 4 serving (1 protein, 1 vegetable)

Spaghetti & Meat Sauce

Ingredients
1lb leanest ground beef, chicken or turkey breast
8 ounces organic tomato sauce (no sugar)
2 cups chopped tomatoes
2 cloves garlic crushed and minced
1/2 cup onion, chopped
1/2 cup celery, chopped
1 teaspoon dried or fresh basil
1 tsp Mrs. Dash Italian Medley
1 teaspoon dried oregano
Sea Salt and black pepper to taste
MCT oil (for sauté)

Directions: Cook the ground meat and drain off excess oil. Add tomato sauce, chopped tomatoes, onion, celery, garlic, and herbs. Simmer on low heat for about 20 minutes. Serve with *Miracle Noodle* Angel Hair pasta.
Modifications: Add 1/4 cup black olives, chopped.
Makes 1 serving (1 protein, 1 vegetable)

Stuffed Cabbage Rolls

Ingredients
1lb lean ground beef, chicken or turkey
12 cabbage leaves*
1 can (15 oz) Tomato sauce (no salt or sugar)
1 medium onion, chopped (about 1/2 cup)
1/2 cup sliced mushrooms
1 cup low sodium beef or chicken broth
1/4 tsp of garlic powder
Dash of onion powder
1 tsp Sea Salt
1/8 tsp Pepper
1 tsp Bragg Liquid Aminos
MCT oil (for frying)

Directions: Preheat oven to 375. Cover cabbage leaves with boiling water and let stand until leaves are limp, about 10 minutes. remove leaves; drain. Spray frying pan with MCT oil combine ground beef, chicken or turkey, onion, mushrooms, garlic and spices and cook until brown. Spoon ground beef mixture (add Miracle Noodle "Rice" to mixture if you want) into cabbage leaves, tuck in ends and roll up (burrito style). Put cabbage rolls in a baking dish and add Braggs to broth and add to the bottom of the pan. Spoon tomato sauce over rolls and bake in oven for 20-30 minutes. Spoon sauce over cabbage rolls periodically to keep moist. *To separate leaves from cabbage head, remove core and cover cabbage with cold water. Let stand about 10 minutes; remove leaves. Modifications: Add 1/2 cup *Miracle Noodle* Rice.
Makes 4 servings (1 protein, 1 vegetable)

SEAFOOD ENTREES

Asian Grilled Shrimp Wraps

Ingredients
100 grams shrimp
1 or more cabbage or lettuce leaves
1 slice fresh ginger
1 tsp apple cider vinegar (ACV)
1 tsp Bragg liquid aminos
1 clove garlic crushed and minced
1/2 tsp Chinese 5 spice powder
1 tsp sesame seeds
1 tablespoon finely minced green onion
stevia (sweeten to taste)
1 tsp MCT oil

Directions: Lightly steam cabbage leaves and then set aside. Combine all ingredients except shrimp in a medium bowl and mix thoroughly. Add shrimp and toss to coat. Cover and refrigerate for 30 minutes. Preheat grill to high or broil in oven. Remove shrimp from marinade, reserving the liquid, and place directly on grill. Cook 1 to 2 minutes each side, until color turns pink. Place reserved marinade in a small saucepan, removing the ginger slice. Bring to a boil and simmer. Drizzle over cooked shrimp, wrap up shrimp mixture in cabbage or lettuce leaves and serve. Modifications: Serve this slightly sweet, grilled shrimp over Miracle Noodles with a side of greens, such as sautéed broccoli. Variations: Dip wraps in Sweet wasabi dipping sauce or top with additional Bragg's. Makes 1 serving (1 protein, 1 vegetable)

Asian Shrimp Salad

Ingredients
100 grams medium shrimp, unpeeled
1 cup water
1/4 cup fresh bean sprouts
1/4 cup sliced water chestnuts, drained
1/8 cup green onions
1/8 cup chopped celery
1 tablespoon lemon juice
1 tsp Bragg liquid aminos
1/8 teaspoon ground ginger
Lettuce or greens of your choice

Directions: In large pot, bring water to a boil. Add shrimp and cook 4 minutes, until shrimp turn pink. Drain shrimp and rinse with cold water. Place in refrigerator until chilled, then peel, devein, and chop the shrimp. In a medium mixing bowl, combine cooked shrimp, bean sprouts, water chestnuts, green onions, and celery. In a separate small mixing bowl, combine lemon juice, Bragg's, and ginger; stir thoroughly. Add to shrimp mixture; toss gently, cover and chill, then top over lettuce or greens of your choice. Makes 1 serving (1 protein)

Baked Fish

Ingredients
4- 6oz any white fish or salmon
1 tsp onion, grated or rings
2 tablespoons lemon juice
1/2 tsp dried dill
1/2 tsp Sea Salt
Dash pepper to taste
MCT oil (for baking)

Directions: Spray baking pan with MCT oil, sprinkle with salt and pepper. Mix lemon juice & onion. Baste fish with mixture and add to baking pan; sprinkle top of fish with salt, pepper and dill. Pour remaining lemon juice mix over fish, cover with foil and cook in oven at 350 degrees. Cook fish for 15-25 minutes or until fish flakes easily with fork. Serve with lemon and top with parsley and onions if desired.
Makes one serving (1 protein)

Baked Mahi Mahi

Ingredients
4 oz fillet mahi mahi fish
1 clove garlic, minced
1 roma tomato, chopped
1 TBS lemon juice
1 drop hot sauce, or to taste
1 tablespoon green onion, chopped
1 TBS MCT oil with Butter Buds
Sea salt to taste

Directions: Preheat an oven to 450 degrees F (230 degrees C). Spray the mahi mahi

fillets with MCT oil and lay into a baking dish. Bake in the preheated oven until the fish flakes easily with a fork, about 20 minutes. While the mahi mahi bakes, mix the MCT oil with butter buds and stir in garlic, lemon juice, and hot sauce; simmer together for 1 minute. Add the tomato and green onion to the mixture; cook and stir until hot. Spoon over the baked fish to serve. Serve on a bed of steamed spinach or greens.
Makes 1 serving (1 protein, 1 fruit)

Baked Orange Roughy Italiano

Ingredients
4 oz orange roughy fish fillet
1 tomato, seeded & chopped
1/4 cup onion, chopped
1 clove garlic, minced
1/4 tsp oregano fresh chopped or dried
1 TBS tomato paste (sugar free)
½ cup low sodium vegetable broth
MCT oil with Butter Buds
Sea salt & ground pepper to taste
1/4 tsp thyme, fresh chopped or dried

Directions: Preheat oven to 350. Spray skillet with MCT oil. Sauté onions and garlic in MCT oil & Butter Buds until soft about 5 minutes. Stir in tomato and seasonings, cover and simmer for 5 minutes, then add the fish, cover with sauce and pour vegetable broth over fish. Cover and bake 15-20 minutes, or until fish flakes with a fork. Remove fish to platter. Simmer sauce in skillet, stir in tomato paste, pour hot over fish. Garnish with parsley. Makes 1 serving (1 protein, 1 vegetable)

Baked Tomato Sole

Ingredients
1 (4-6 oz) sole or catfish fillet
1 small onion, thinly sliced
1 plum tomato, sliced
2 tablespoons butter or margarine, melted
1/8 teaspoon garlic powder
1/8 tsp Sea salt
Dash pepper
2 TBS MCT oil & Butter Buds
MCT oil (for sauté)
2 tablespoons fresh parsley, minced

Directions: Sauté onion in MCT oil until tender. Transfer to a greased baking dish (spray with MCT oil). Place fillet over onions. Sprinkle with salt and pepper. Top with tomato slices. Combine MCT, butter buds and garlic powder; then pour over tomato. Sprinkle with parsley. Bake, uncovered, at 350 degrees F for 14-18 minutes or until fish flakes easily with a fork. Makes 1 serving (1 protein)

Blackened Fish

Ingredients
4-6oz piece red snapper, tilapia or salmon
2 1/2 teaspoons paprika
1 teaspoon dried thyme
1 teaspoon onion powder
1 teaspoon garlic powder
3/4 teaspoon cayenne pepper
1/4 teaspoon dried oregano
½ teaspoon dried basil
Juice of 1 lemon
1 1/2 teaspoons sea salt
1/2 tsp black pepper & 1/2 tsp white pepper
MCT oil (for frying)

Directions: Preheat oven 400. Mix spices well in shaker jar. Dip fish in lemon juice, spray fish with MCT oil then dip fish in enough of the spice mixture to coat pieces of fish thoroughly. Preheat skillet to high heat (spray with MCT Oil. Add fish dry and cook quickly until spices are blackened about 2 minutes each side. Then bake in oven for about 8 minutes or when fish flakes easily with fork. Serve hot. Garnish with lemon and fresh parsley. Save the rest of the blackened spice mixture to use later. Works well with chicken also. Makes 1 serving (1 protein)

Broiled Lobster Tails

Ingredients
1 raw lobster tail
1/4 tsp paprika
MCT oil & Butter Buds
Sea salt and white pepper to taste
1 wedge lemon

Directions: Preheat the broiler and place the lobster tail on baking sheet. With a sharp knife or kitchen shears, carefully cut top side of lobster shell lengthwise. Pull shell apart slightly and spray MCT oil on meat, then season with butter buds, paprika, salt, and white pepper. Broil lobster tails until lightly browned and lobster meat is opaque, about 5 to 10 minutes. Garnish with lemon wedge. Makes 1 serving (1 protein)

Broiled Scallops

Ingredients
100 grams bay scallops
1 tablespoon garlic powder

2 tablespoons lemon, juiced
1 TBS MCT oil & Butter Buds (mix)
1 tsp sea salt

Directions: Turn broiler on. Rinse scallops and place in broiling pan. Sprinkle with garlic, salt, MCT & butter buds mixture and lemon juice. Broil 6 to 8 minutes or until scallops start to turn golden. Remove from oven and serve with extra MCT and Butter Buds mixture on the side for dipping. Makes 1 serving (1 protein)

Cajun Jambalaya

Ingredients
1 lb shrimp (chicken, beef, or chicken sausage can be used or a combination)
1 tomato, chopped
1/4 cup celery, diced
1/4 cup green bell pepper, diced
1/4 cup onion, chopped
1 cup low sodium vegetable or chicken broth
2 tablespoons lemon juice
2 bay leaves
2 cloves garlic crushed and minced
1 tsp Bragg liquid aminos
Dash of hot sauce
1/4 tsp cayenne powder
1/8 teaspoon onion powder
Sea salt and pepper to taste
MCT oil (for browning)

Directions: Heat oil in a large pot over medium high heat. Sauté shrimp, chicken and/or meats until lightly browned, about 5 minutes (shrimp with be pink). Stir in tomato, onion, bell pepper, celery and garlic. Season with cayenne, onion powder, salt and pepper. Cook 5 minutes, or until onion is tender and translucent. Then stir in vegetable or chicken stock and bay leaves. Bring to a boil, then reduce heat, cover, and simmer 10-20 minutes or until meats are thoroughly cooked. Stir in the Braggs and hot sauce to flavor. Makes 4 servings (1 protein, 1 vegetable, 1 fruit)

Garlic Shrimp Scampi

Ingredients

100 grams shrimp
1/4 cup low sodium vegetable broth
2 cloves garlic crushed and minced
1 TBS green onion, minced
Pinch of paprika
Sea salt to taste
MCT oil (for sauté)

Directions: Spray frying pan with MCT oil. Sauté the shrimp in broth and garlic for about 3 minutes or until cooked through (shrimp will be opaque). Season with salt, green onion and paprika. Makes 1 serving (1 protein)
Serve with *Miracle Noodle* Rice or Pasta

Grilled Shrimp On A Skewer

Ingredients
100 grams large shrimp, peeled & deveined
1 large garlic clove, minced
1 tsp sea salt
1/4 teaspoon paprika
1/8 teaspoon cayenne
2 tsp MCT oil
1 teaspoons fresh lemon juice
Freshly sliced lemons, for garnish

Directions: Soak wooden skewers in cold water for 1 hr. In a medium bowl, mix garlic, salt, paprika, and cayenne. Add oil and lemon juice; mix to form a paste. Add shrimp, cover, and marinate for 2 hours. Preheat grill to high heat. Remove shrimp from marinade and place on skewer and then on grill; cook 2 minutes per side, until shrimp turn pink. Serve as an appetizer or with salad. Garnish lemon wedges. Variation: Sauté in pan. Makes 1 serving (1 protein)

Italian Shrimp & Zucchini

Ingredients
100 grams shrimp
2 large tomatoes chopped
1 small zucchini, chopped
¼ cup low sodium vegetable broth
1 tablespoons lemon juice
¼ teaspoon dried or fresh basil
2 cloves of garlic crushed and minced
1/2 tsp Mrs. Dash Italian Medley
Pinch of dried or fresh oregano

MCT oil (for sauté)
Sea salt and black pepper to taste

Directions: Sauté onion, garlic and spices in broth and lemon juice. Add zucchini and cook for 5 minutes. Add the shrimp and tomatoes and cook until shrimp is pink and well cooked. Makes 1 serving (1 protein, 1 vegetable)

Lemon-Orange Roughy Fish

Ingredients
4 oz orange roughy fish fillet
1 orange slice
1 lemon slice
1 TBS lemon, juiced
1 TBS orange, juiced
1/4 tsp lemon pepper
Sea salt to taste
1 tsp MCT oil

Directions: Heat oil in a large skillet over medium-high heat. Arrange fillet in the skillet, and drizzle with orange juice and lemon juice. Sprinkle with lemon pepper and sea salt. Cook for 5 minutes, or until fish is easily flaked with a fork. Garnish with lemon and orange wedges. Makes 1 serving (1 protein, 1 fruit)

Onion Caramelized Shrimp

Ingredients
100 grams shrimp
Sliced onion cut into rings
¼ cup water
3 tablespoons lemon juice
1 tablespoons Bragg's liquid aminos
1/4 tsp Mrs. Dash Onion Herb
Vanilla flavored liquid stevia to taste
Sea salt and pepper to taste
MCT oil (for frying)

Directions: Heat up the liquid ingredients on high heat in small frying pan. Add stevia, salt, pepper, onion, herbs and shrimp. Deglaze with a little water several times to create a caramelized sauce. Makes 1 serving (1 protein, 1 vegetable)

Pan Seared Ginger Red Snapper

Ingredients
2 (4 oz) red snapper fillets
1 lemon, juiced

2 TBS apple cider vinegar (ACV)
1 tsp Dijon mustard
1 tsp ground ginger
1/4 cup green onions, chopped
1 TBS MCT oil (for sauté)
pinch of stevia
Sea salt and fresh ground pepper to taste

Directions: Rinse snapper under cold water, and pat dry. In a shallow bowl, mix together MCT oil, lemon juice, ACV, mustard, stevia, green onions, and ginger. Heat a non-stick skillet over medium heat, spray with MCT oil. Dip snapper fillets in marinade to coat both sides, and place in skillet. Cook for 2 to 3 minutes on each side. Pour remaining marinade into skillet. Reduce heat, and simmer for 2 to 3 minutes, or until fish flakes easily with a fork. Makes 1 serving (1 protein)

Poached Salmon Piccata

Ingredients
8 oz Salmon Fillet (or 2- 4oz)
½ cup vegetable or chicken broth
2 tablespoons capers
2 tablespoons lemon juice
1TBS fresh parsley, chopped
1 tsp MCT oil & Butter Buds
Sea salt and black pepper to taste

Directions: Bring broth and lemon juice to boil in medium-sized skillet, reduce heat to simmer and add salmon fillet to pan. Cover and simmer over low heat, 10 minutes per inch of thickness (measure at thickest part), or until fish flakes easily with fork. Remove salmon from pan and keep warm. Boil remaining liquid in skillet, whisk in MCT, butter buds and capers. Spoon over fish, Season with salt and pepper and sprinkle with parsley. Makes 2 servings (1 protein)

Poached Halibut Fillet

Ingredients
4oz halibut fillet
1/2 cup low sodium vegetable broth
1 TBS capers
1 tablespoon lemon juice
1 tablespoon chopped onion
1/8 cup flat leaf parsley (fresh)
½ lemon (thinly sliced rounds)
Sea salt and pepper to taste
MCT oil

Directions: Chop capers and pat fish dry. Sprinkle fish with salt and pepper and let stand at room temperature for 10 minutes. Arrange half the lemon slices in 1 layer in MCT sprayed 8 inch glass baking dish. Arrange fish over lemon, top with lemon juice, capers, onion, remaining lemon slices and parsley, then pour broth over fish. Bake in the middle of oven, uncovered until fish flakes and is cooked through 30-45 minutes. Serve topped with remaining juices as a sauce and top with parsley.
Makes one serving (1 protein)

Sautéed White Fish

Ingredients
100 grams of any white fish (cod, halibut, etc)
2 cloves garlic crushed and minced
1 TBS MCT oil (for sauté)
Sea Salt and black pepper to taste

Directions: Cut fish into bite size pieces. Sauté fish in MCT oil, garlic, salt & pepper for 3-4 minutes each side or until fish is completely cooked (easily flakes with fork). Garnish with lemon wedges.
Variations: Use Olive oil on Maintenance. Makes 1 serving (1 protein)

Shrimp & Asparagus Salad

Ingredients
1/4 pound bay salad shrimp
1/4 pound asparagus, break off hard ends
1 TBS extra-virgin olive oil or MCT oil
1 garlic clove, minced
1 Tbsp lemon juice (more to taste)
1 Tbsp minced fresh parsley
Sea Salt and black pepper to taste

Directions: Bring a medium pot of water to a boil. Add the asparagus to the boiling

water and boil for 3 minutes. Use a slotted spoon to remove the asparagus to a bowl to cool. Slice the asparagus spears thinly on the diagonal until you get close to the tip. Cut the asparagus tips off in one piece. (They look prettier that way.) Put the asparagus in the bowl with the shrimp. Add the remaining ingredients and toss to combine. Add salt and black pepper to taste. Add more lemon juice if desired, to taste.
Makes 1 serving (1 protein, 1 vegetable)

Shrimp Creole

Ingredients
100 grams shrimp, peeled & deveined
½ cup low sodium vegetable broth or water
1 clove garlic crushed and minced
1 tablespoon onion, minced
¼ cup green bell pepper, chopped
1/4 cup celery, chopped
1 clove garlic, minced
1/2 cup tomatoes, diced
1 TBS tomato paste (no sugar)
1/4 tsp cayenne pepper
1-2 teaspoons hot sauce to taste
1 tablespoons lemon juice
1 tsp Bragg liquid aminos
1 bay leaf
Pinch of Cajun Seasoning
Sea Salt to taste
1 TBS fresh parsley, chopped
MCT oil (for frying)

Directions: Spray pan with MCT oil over medium heat. Add onion, bell pepper, garlic, and celery and sauté until tender. Add tomatoes, tomato paste, liquid ingredients, bay leaf and spices and bring to boil. Cover, reduce heat and simmer over low heat for 10 minutes in frying pan. Add shrimp and cook for an additional 5 minutes until shrimp is opaque and cooked through, add salt if needed. Serve with parsley, hot or cold over a salad or *Miracle Noodle* rice.
Makes 1 serving (1 protein)

Shrimp Curry

Ingredients
1lb of large shrimp, peeled and deveined
1 green pepper, chopped into 1/2 in pieces
1 large onion, chopped
1 one-inch cinnamon stick
6 green cardamom pods
6 cloves

1 bay leaf
2 green chilies, chopped
1 tsp ginger root, minced
1 tsp garlic, minced
1 tsp cumin, ground
1 tsp coriander, ground
½ tsp Sea salt
3 TBS MCT oil
1 ½ cups canned tomatoes, crushed
2 sprigs fresh cilantro, chopped

Directions: Heat oil over medium in a large skillet. Add onion and cook until tender, 4 to 5 minutes. Add cinnamon, cardamom, cloves, and bay leaf; cook an additional minute. Add chilies, ginger, garlic, cumin, coriander, and salt; cook additional 30 seconds. Add green pepper and tomatoes, then bring to a boil over high heat. Add shrimp, lower to a simmer, and cook 15 minutes, covered. Sprinkle with cilantro and serve over *Miracle Noodle* rice.
Makes 1 serving (1 protein)

Shrimp & Grapefruit Salad

Ingredients
100 grams medium shrimp, shelled
1 tsp Bragg Liquid Aminos
1/8 teaspoon cayenne red pepper, ground
1 tablespoon low sodium vegetable stock or water
1 cup fresh spinach leaves, torn into bite-size pieces
1/2 pink grapefruit, peeled and sectioned
1 scallion, thinly sliced
1 TBS apple cider vinegar (ACV)
1 tsp MCT oil
dash of stevia
Sea salt

Directions: Bring large pot of salted water to a boil. Add shrimp and cook until pink, 2 to 3 minutes. Drain and allow to cool. In a small bowl, make the dressing by whisking together the MCT oil, stevia, ACV, Braggs, cayenne, and stock. Arrange spinach leaves on a serving platter; sprinkle with a few tablespoons of dressing. Position the grapefruit sections and cooked shrimp over spinach and drizzle with the remaining dressing. Garnish with scallions.
Makes 1 serving (1 protein, 1 vegetable)

Sweet and Sour Shrimp

Ingredients
100 grams shrimp

1 cup water
½ lemon with rind
½ orange with rind
3 tablespoons Bragg's liquid aminos
1 tablespoon minced onion
1 clove garlic crushed and minced
Cayenne to taste
Salt and pepper to taste
MCT oil (for sauté)
Stevia to taste

Directions: Boil 1 cup of water with ½ lemon and ½ orange with rind until pulp comes out of the center. Scrape out remaining pulp and discard the rind. Add onion, garlic, Bragg's, and spices and reduce liquid by half. Add the shrimp to the sauce and sauté for 5-7 minutes until shrimp is cooked.
Makes 1 serving (1 protein, 1 fruit)
Modifications: Add red and green bell peppers to the mix.

Tilapia Taco's

Ingredients
1 (6oz) Tilapia fish fillet
yellow & orange peppers, cut in long strips
1/2 cup tomato, diced
1 tsp ground chipotle seasoning
1/4 tsp ground cumin
2 tsp MCT oil
1/4 teaspoon grated lime rind
1 tablespoons fresh lime juice
Sea salt to taste
MCT oil (spray)
Lettuce leaves

Directions: Combine chipotle, cumin & salt. Rub seasoning mixture evenly over fillet. Stir together oil, grated rind, and juice; rub over fillets. Arrange fillets in a grill basket coated with cooking spray. Grill over medium-high heat (350° to 400°) 3 minutes on each side or just until fish begins to flake with a fork. Cool slightly. Shred fish. Spoon 2 to 3 tablespoons fish into lettuce leaves (mach taco), and top with peppers & tomato. Variations: top with Dana's Salsa. Serve with a squeeze of fresh lime juice.
Makes 1 serving (1 protein)

VEGETABLES

Artichoke Italiano

Ingredients
1 globe artichoke
1 TBS lemon juice
2 cloves garlic, minced
1 tablespoon olive oil or MCT oil

Directions: This is my Papa's recipe. Slice about 1 inch off the tip of the artichoke. If the artichokes have little thorns on the end of the leaves, take a kitchen scissors and cut of the thorned tips of all of the leaves. This step is mostly for aesthetics as the thorns soften with cooking and pose no threat to the person eating the artichoke, if I'm lazy I leave those on. Pull off any smaller leaves towards the base and on the stem. Cut off stem, so artichoke sits upright. The stems tend to be more bitter than the rest of the artichoke, but I like to eat them. Rinse the artichokes in cold running water. In a large pot, put a couple inches of water, artichokes, garlic, lemon juice, and drizzle with oil. Cover. Bring to a boil and reduce heat to simmer. Cook for 25 to 45 minutes or until the outer leaves can easily be pulled off. Note: Cooking time depends on how large the artichoke is, the larger, the longer it takes to cook and you can over cook and the leaves get a little tougher. Artichokes may be eaten cold or hot, but I think they are much better hot. I grew up on them and like them plain, but you could dip leaves in either MCT oil & Butter buds or melted butter. To eat: Pull off outer petals, one at a time. Dip white fleshy end in dip or eat plain. Tightly grip the other end of the petal. Place in mouth, dip side down, and pull through teeth to remove soft, pulpy, delicious portion of the petal. Discard remaining petal. Continue until all petals are removed. With a knife or spoon, scrape out and discard the inedible fuzzy part (called the "choke") covering the artichoke heart. The remaining bottom of the artichoke is the heart. Cut into pieces and eat plain or dip into melted butter or MCT oil with Butter buds for buttery flavor.
Makes 1 servings (1 vegetable)

Asparagus & Spinach Salad

Ingredients
3 cups fresh spinach leaves

6 fresh asparagus spears
1/8 cup MCT oil
2 TBS lemon juice
2 TBS Parmesan cheese, grated
1 tablespoon slivered almonds

Directions: Combine lemon juice and MCT oil on plate. Dip asparagus and roll around to coat. Grill or sauté asparagus for about 5 minutes, turning at least once over medium heat, and brushing with oil & lemon mixture. Remove from the grill or pan, and place back onto the plate with the oil mixture. In a large bowl, combine the spinach, Parmesan cheese, and slivered almonds. Cut asparagus into bite size pieces, and add to the salad along with the lemon juice and oil from the plate. Toss to blend, then serve. Add tomatoes if desired! Makes 3 servings (1 vegetable)

Baked Rainbow Chard & Feta

Ingredients
1 bunch rainbow chard - leaves and stems separated and chopped
1 medium sweet onion, chopped
1 tablespoon MCT oil
Sea salt and black pepper to taste
2 tablespoons MCT oil
4 ounces feta cheese, broken into 1/2 inch pieces

Directions: Preheat an oven to 350 degrees F. Spray MCT oil on baking sheet. Toss the chard stems and onions in a bowl with 1 tablespoon MCT oil. Season with salt and pepper to taste, and spread on baking sheet. Bake in the preheated oven until the chard stems have softened and the onion is starting to brown on the corners, about 15 minutes. Toss the chard leaves with 2 tablespoons MCT oil, salt, and black pepper. Sprinkle the leaves over the stem mixture, then scatter the feta cheese over top. Return to the oven, and bake until the stems are tender, the leaves are beginning to crisp, and the feta is melted and golden, about 20 minutes. Makes 1-2 servings (1 vegetable)

Beet Greens with Tomato & Onions

Ingredients
2 cups beet greens, chopped
2 tablespoons MCT oil
1/2 small white onion, chopped
1 small tomato, chopped
1 large clove garlic, minced
1/4 teaspoon ground thyme
1/8 teaspoon red pepper flakes
1/4 cup water
2 tablespoons apple cider vinegar (ACV)
Sea salt & ground black pepper to taste

Directions: Heat MCT oil in a large skillet over medium heat; cook and stir onion in hot oil until browned, about 10 minutes. Add beet greens, tomato, and garlic. Continue cooking until beet greens are wilted. Sprinkle thyme and red pepper flakes over vegetables. Stir in water, ACV, salt, and pepper. Makes 4 Servings (1 vegetable)

Big Vegetable Salad

Ingredients
Handful Spinach and/or Romaine, chopped
1 celery stalk, chopped
1 slice sweet onion, chopped
1/4 cup cucumber, chopped
1/4 cup tomatoes, chopped
2-3 radishes, sliced
1 TBS apple cider vinegar (ACV)
1 TBS MCT oil

Directions: Place spinach and/or lettuce in bowl and top with desired vegetables and protein of your choice (tuna, chicken, steak, etc). Drizzle dressing. Add lemon or Bragg liquid amino's for more flavor! Makes 1 serving (1 vegetable)

Broiled Sweet Mini Peppers

Ingredients
Bag of tri-colored sweet mini peppers
(red, orange & yellow)
MCT oil or Olive oil

Directions: Spray MCT oil on baking pan (cookie sheet). Place the mini peppers in rows to fill. Drizzle lightly or spray oil over peppers. Broil until brown and then with thongs flip peppers and broil on other side until brown. Delicious sweet snacks! Makes 1 or more servings (1 vegetable)

Cabbage Soup

Ingredients
Chopped cabbage (½ head)
1 large tomato, chopped
2 cups low sodium chicken broth or water
1/4 cup onion finely chopped
1 clove garlic crushed and minced
Sea Salt and pepper to taste
2 tsp Bragg liquid aminos
MCT oil (for frying)

Directions: In a large frying pan, heat chicken broth, onion, garlic, salt and Braggs. Add cabbage and tomato cover pan with a lid. Cook cabbage until tender.
Makes 1-2 servings (1 vegetable)

Celery with Salsa

Ingredients
Celery, washed and cut
Dana's Salsa (see recipe)

Directions: Chop up celery into sticks. Dip into Dana's Salsa
Makes 1-2 servings (1 vegetable)

Cabbage & Shrimp Salad

Ingredients
1 pound cooked shrimp, peeled and deveined
1 head cabbage, diced
4 celery stalks, diced
2 green onions, thinly sliced
1/2 cup Apple cider Vinegar
1/4 cup MCT oil
stevia to taste

Directions: Gently mix the shrimp, cabbage, celery, and green onions together in a large bowl. Stir the ACV, MCT oil and stevia together in a separate bowl; add to the shrimp mixture and gently stir until all ingredients are evenly coated. Refrigerate for 3 hours to allow the cabbage to soften and the flavors to blend.
Makes 4 or more servings (1 vegetable, 1 protein)

Chicory & Orange Salad

Ingredients
2 cups chopped fresh chicory (curly endive)
1 medium navel orange
1/8 cup red onion, finely minced
2 teaspoons apple cider or red wine vinegar
1 tablespoon Bragg's liquid aminos
1 tablespoon lemon juice
Sea salt and pepper to taste

Directions: Chop chicory very fine, add onion. Cut and peel oranges crosswise into 1/4 inch size pieces. Stir in apple cider vinegar, Bragg's and lemon juice. Add salt and fresh ground black pepper to taste. Enjoy as a side dish or cool salad.
Makes 1 serving (1 vegetable, 1 fruit)

Fennel & Cucumber Salsa

Ingredients
1 large Fennel bulb, diced
1 cucumber, diced
1 avocado - peeled, pitted, and diced
1/2 red onion, chopped
1/4 cup green chili peppers
1 bunch cilantro, chopped
2 tablespoons honey or stevia to taste
3 tablespoons fresh lemon juice
Sea salt and pepper to taste

Directions: Combine the cucumber, fennel, avocado, red onion, green chili peppers, cilantro, stevia or honey, lemon juice, salt, and pepper in a bowl. Allow mixture to sit 20 minutes before serving. Dip with celery, use on grilled meats, taco salads, etc
Makes 1 or more servings (1 vegetable)

Garlic Cabbage Salad

Ingredients

1 small head of cabbage finely chopped
1 tablespoon water, or as needed
1 small green bell pepper, chopped
1 cucumber, thinly sliced
1/4 cup apple cider vinegar
2 teaspoons garlic powder
2 teaspoons Sea salt
1 celery stalk, shredded
2 small tomatoes, cut into wedges
1/2 cup MCT Oil

Directions: Place garlic powder into a bowl. Stir in enough water to make a runny paste. Toss in the cabbage, bell pepper, celery, cucumber, and tomatoes until well coated. Let stand for 10 minutes. Whisk together the vinegar, MCT oil, and salt in a bowl. Pour dressing over the prepared vegetables. Mix thoroughly, then cover and refrigerate overnight. Makes 8 servings (1 vegetable)

Italian Asparagus Salad

Ingredients
1 lb fresh Asparagus, trimmed & cut into 1 1/2 inch pieces
4 plum tomatoes, halved and sliced
1/2 cup chopped red onion
2 TBS apple cider vinegar (ACV)
2 tablespoons lemon juice
1 clove of garlic crushed and minced
2 tablespoons MCT oil
Parmesan cheese

Directions: Place asparagus in a steamer or place in a saucepan over 1 in. of water. Bring to a boil; cover and steam for 5-7 minutes or until crisp-tender. Drain and immediately place asparagus in ice water. Drain and pat dry. In a large bowl, combine the asparagus, tomatoes and onion. Mix ACV, lemon juice, garlic and MCT oil and gently toss to coat. Sprinkle with parmesan cheese. Serve as side dish, on lettuce or with favorite meat dish. Makes 4 servings (1 vegetable)

Mashed Cauli-tatoes

Ingredients
1 large head of cauliflower
1 TBS MCT oil (or olive oil)
1/3 cup whole organic milk
Sea salt & pepper to taste
Butter Buds to taste

Directions: Cut cauliflower into 4-6 pieces and steam until cooked but not over done. Put in blender or food processor with remaining ingredients and blend until the consistency of mashed potatoes. Serve immediately. Makes 4 servings (1 vegetable)

Onions & Burger

Ingredients
½ red or sweet onion cut into rings
Sea salt & pepper to taste
1 TBS Bragg liquid aminos
Protein Burgers (leanest ground beef or ground turkey breast) of your choice
Spray pan with MCT oil

Directions: Spray skillet with MCT oil. Fry burger of your choice with salt & pepper to taste. Alongside burgers in skillet, add onion and Braggs, let the juices cover the onions as they sauté along side meat for added flavor. When cooked top meat with onion! Makes 4 servings (1 vegetable, 1 protein)

Pesto Tomato & Cucumber Salad

Ingredients
2 medium tomatoes or 3 Roma tomatoes sliced.
1 medium cucumber, sliced
1+ TBS Pesto (see Papa's Pesto recipe)
1 tablespoon of apple cider vinegar

Directions: Toss fresh tomatoes & cucumbers with Papa's Pesto and ACV. Marinate for at least 1 hour. Top with fresh basil or Italian parsley and serve.
2-3 servings (1 vegetable or fruit)

Radish & Cucumber Salad

Ingredients
1 cup radishes, sliced
1/4 teaspoon sea salt
1/4 cup sliced red onion
1/2 cup sliced cucumber
2 TBS MCT oil
2 tablespoons apple cider vinegar
1 clove garlic, minced
1/2 teaspoon chopped fresh dill
stevia to taste

Directions: Toss radishes with red onion and cucumber slices. Whisk MCT oil, ACV, salt, garlic, and dill in a small bowl until well mixed; pour over vegetables and toss to combine. Cover and refrigerate for at least 1 hour before serving. Add stevia for desired sweetness. Makes 2 servings (1 vegetable)

Sautéed Garlic Spinach

Ingredients
1 lb of fresh or frozen Spinach
½ cup low sodium chicken broth or water
2 tablespoons lemon juice
2 tablespoons onion, minced
2 cloves garlic crushed and minced
¼ tsp Mrs. Dash Garlic Herb
Pinch red pepper flakes
MCT oil (for sauté)

Directions: Sauté the onion and garlic lightly in frying pan with MCT oil, a little water and lemon juice until soft. Add fresh garlic and spices. Stir in fresh spinach leaves and cook lightly. Serve with your favorite chicken or fish dish.
Makes 1-2 servings (1 vegetable)

Steamed Asparagus

Ingredients

1 lb fresh Asparagus, trimmed
1 cup water
Sea salt & pepper to taste
Butter Buds or Natural Yeast to taste

Directions: In a large skillet, bring water to a boil; add asparagus. Cover and cook for 4-6 minutes or until almost tender; drain and pat dry. Cool slightly. Add salt and pepper and/or Butter Buds or Natural Yeast to taste. Makes 1 serving (1 vegetable)

Sautéed Cabbage

Ingredients
3 cups chopped cabbage
1/2 medium onion, chopped
2 tablespoons MCT oil
2 celery stalks, thinly sliced
1/4 cup low sodium organic chicken broth
1/2 teaspoon sea salt
Stevia to taste

Directions: In a large skillet, sauté onion in MCT oil until tender. Add celery; cook and stir for 2-3 minutes. Stir in the remaining ingredients; bring to a boil. Reduce heat; cover and simmer for 5-7 minutes or until vegetables are tender.
Makes 3 servings (1 vegetable)

Sesame Spinach

Ingredients
Fresh or frozen Bag of Spinach
1 TBS Sesame Seeds
1 tsp Bragg's Liquid Aminos
1 tsp Apple Cider Vinegar (ACV)
1 tsp MCT Oil
Sea Salt to taste

Directions: Steam spinach. Drain as much excess water as possible. Add MCT oil, sesame seeds and Liquid Aminos and/or ACV. I like one or the other and sometimes both! Can eat warm or refrigerate. Makes 1-2 servings (1 vegetable)

Spinach & Strawberry Salad

Ingredients
10 oz fresh Spinach, rinse, dried & torn into bite-size pieces
2 tablespoons sesame seeds
1 tablespoon poppy seeds
1/4 cup MCT oil
1/4 cup apple cider vinegar (ACV)
1/4 teaspoon paprika
1/4 teaspoon Bragg liquid aminos
1 tablespoon onion, minced
1 quart strawberries, washed, topped and sliced
1/4 cup almonds, slivered
1/8 tsp Vanilla Stevia

Directions: In a medium bowl, whisk together the sesame seeds, poppy seeds, stevia, MCT oil, ACV, paprika, Braggs and onion. Cover, and chill for one hour. In a large bowl, combine the spinach, strawberries and almonds. Pour dressing over salad, and toss. Refrigerate 10 to 15 minutes before serving.
Makes 4 servings (1 vegetable, 1 fruit)

Teriyaki Onion Topper

Ingredients
½ large onion cut into fine rings
1 TBS Bragg Liquid Aminos
Small amount of water as needed
Pinch of sea salt
MCT oil

Directions: Preheat skillet. Spray pan with MCT oil. Add small amount of water to bottom of pan and Braggs. Add onion rings and cook quickly periodically deglazing the pan with a little more water to create a teriyaki sauce. Serve immediately over steak or chicken. Makes 4 servings (1 vegetable)

Tomato Salad

Ingredients
2 medium tomatoes, cut in wedges
¼ cup apple cider vinegar
1 tablespoon green onion, chopped
1 garlic clove crushed and minced
1 tsp Mrs. Dash Tomato Basil
1 teaspoon MCT oil

Salt and pepper to taste

Directions: Combine apple cider vinegar with, garlic, oil & spices. Pour over tomato chunks or slices. Marinate and chill for 1 hour before serving. Top with Green onion. Makes 2 servings (1 vegetable)

Tomato & Green Pepper Salad

Ingredients
2 medium tomatoes, chopped
1 medium green pepper, chopped
1 celery stalk, thinly sliced
1/4 cup chopped red or sweet onion
1 tablespoons apple cider vinegar (ACV)
Sea Salt and black pepper to taste

Directions: In a large bowl, combine the tomatoes, green pepper, celery and onion. In a small bowl, combine the ACV, salt and pepper. Stir into tomato mixture. Cover and refrigerate for at least 2 hours, stirring several times. Makes 4 servings (1 vegetable)

Tomatoes Grilled

Ingredients
2 firm, ripe tomatoes (not overly ripe)
MCT oil or Olive oil
4 basil leaves, thinly sliced (roll them up like a
Cigar and then slice them to make nice thin slices)
Sea Salt and black pepper to taste

Directions: Gently dislodge and remove the watery pulp and seeds. Preheat grill on high heat for direct grilling. Use a grill basket or fine grill grate if you can. Season with salt and pepper. Brush the cut side of tomato and grill grate or pan with oil. Place the tomatoes, cut side down on the grill surface. Cover the grill and let cook for about 4 minutes. Drizzle a little more oil on the tomatoes. Sprinkle with thinly sliced basil. Makes 2-4 servings (1 vegetable)

DESSERTS

Apple Cinnamon Chips

Ingredients
1 apple
Dash of cinnamon
Powdered Stevia to taste

Directions: Slice apples thinly, mix stevia and cinnamon in small bowl. Dip sliced apples into mix and coat one side (I find that coating both sides is quite strong). Bake at 325 until chewy (a little brown) and a little crispy. Add nutmeg if desired. Make a big batch for snacking! Makes 1 serving (1 fruit)

Apple Custard Pie

Ingredients
4-5 baking apples
1 TBS lemon juice
1/4 tsp Vanilla Stevia or 1/2 c honey
3 eggs
3/4 cup homemade or Greek whole plain yogurt
1/8 teaspoon cinnamon
1/4 tsp nutmeg
1/4 cup apple cider
2-3 TBS almonds or walnuts, chopped

Directions: Core and cut apples into eighths. Toss in lemon juice which has been mixed with stevia or honey. Arrange apple slices round side down in a pie plate with a circle around the outer edge and another circle inside that, filling the center. Bake in oven at 400 for 20 minutes. Beat the eggs slightly, stir in yogurt, apple cider, cinnamon & nutmeg. Pour egg mixture over the apples and continue baking another 10 minutes. Sprinkle the top with the chopped nuts and bake 10 minutes longer or until the top is golden and center firm. Cool on rack before cutting. Makes 4-6 servings (1 fruit)

Baked Walnut Apples

Ingredients
4 large apples for baking, cored and sliced
1/2 teaspoon cinnamon
Pinch of nutmeg
1/4 tsp liquid vanilla stevia to taste
1/4 c walnut pieces

Directions: Choose an apple that bakes well such as McIntosh, Spy, Ida Red. Toss

apples in bowl with spices and stevia to taste. Add walnuts. Bake in 8x8 baking dish, 350 F oven until apples are tender when poked about 20 minutes.
Makes 4-6 servings (1 fruit)

Broiled Grapefruit

Ingredients
1 grapefruit
Powdered stevia to taste

Directions: Cut grapefruit in half, remove seeds. Cut around sections to loosen, remove centers. Sprinkle with stevia. Set oven to broil. Broil fruit 4-6 inches from heat until juice bubbles and edges of peels turn light brown, about 5-10 minutes. Serve hot.
Makes 2 servings (1 fruit)

Berry Sorbet

Ingredients
1 cup fresh berries (strawberries, raspberries or blackberries)
¼ cup pure cranberry juice
1 cup of ice cubes
1/4 tsp Vanilla liquid stevia to taste

Directions: Add all ingredients in high powdered blender, Blend but do not over mix, Serve or place in freezer. Makes two servings (1 fruit)

Coffee Ice Cream

Ingredients
1/4 cup espresso
3 cups ice cubes
1 scoop Vanilla Protein Shake
1 cup water
1/2 cup half and half
stevia to taste

Directions: Blend ingredients together in high powered blender until smooth, do not over mix. Serve or place in the freezer.

Caramel Apple Pie

Ingredients
1 apple
1 tablespoon lemon juice
1 tablespoon water
1 teaspoon apple cider vinegar

1 packet powdered stevia
1 teaspoon ground cinnamon
Pinch of nutmeg
1 tablespoon water
English toffee stevia to taste

Directions: Slice apple into very thin slices. Arrange in layers in a round 3 inch crème Brule dish. For each layer, sprinkle generously with cinnamon, nutmeg, and powdered and English toffee stevia. Continue layering with spices until dish is full. Sprinkle lemon juice, apple cider vinegar and water over the apple slices. Bake at 375 for approximately 20-25 minutes or until apples are cooked and top is slightly crispy. Drizzle with additional English toffee stevia if desired. Serve warm. Makes 1 serving (1 fruit)

Chocolate Covered Strawberries

Ingredients
4-6 medium strawberries
Dana's Easy Chocolate Candy

Directions: Wash strawberries and dip in warm chocolate mixture. Place on wax or parchment paper and place in refrigerator. Variations: Use orange segments.
Makes 1 serving (1 fruit)

Dana's Easy Chocolate Candy

Ingredients
1 cup cocoa powder (regular or dark chocolate)
3/4 cup organic extra-virgin coconut oil

1 tsp vanilla stevia

Directions: Mix cocoa and coconut oil together in small sauce pan over medium heat. When melted, turn off heat, add stevia and stir well. Place mini paper cups in small muffin pan. Scoop 2 teaspoons of chocolate in each cup. Put pan in freezer for about 10 minutes. You will have about 4 batches. After frozen store in refrigerator, if warm they will melt. Variations: Add 1/2 cup crushed almonds or put 2-4 almonds per candy. Makes about 24 servings (1 chocolate craving)

Greek Yogurt A La Fruit

Ingredients
½ cup Greek Yogurt
1/4 cup fruit of your choice (raspberries, blackberries, strawberries)
Powdered stevia to taste

Directions: Mix stevia into yogurt to taste. Top with fruit and sprinkle with stevia. Makes one serving (1 fruit)

Homemade Applesauce with Cinnamon

Ingredients
4 medium cooking apples, cut into fourths
1/2 c water
1/4 teaspoon cinnamon
1/8 tsp nutmeg
1/4 tsp vanilla stevia

Directions: Heat apples and water to boiling over medium heat, reduce, simmer uncovered, stirring occasionally to break up apples, until tender for 5-10 minutes. Add cinnamon, nutmeg and stevia to taste. Serve warm or cold. Makes 4 servings (1 fruit)

Instant Blender Frozen Yogurt

Ingredients
1 cup whole Greek plain yogurt
1/2 cup frozen fruit (strawberries, raspberries, blackberries, orange, lemon or lime)
Powdered stevia to taste (or a little honey)

Directions: Place 1/2 cup yogurt in blender. Gradually add frozen fruit and rest of the yogurt. Add stevia to taste. Blend until thick (you may have to add a bit extra fruit for desired consistency). Store in freezer. It is meant to be eaten soon after making or if refrozen with crystallize. Makes 1 serving (1 fruit)

Protein Soda Shakes

Ingredients
1 scoop vanilla Lean Protein Powder
4-8 oz pure water (depending on desired taste)
3-4 ice cubes (depending on desired thickness)
Any flavored Stevia to taste (root beer, orange, hazelnut, grape or any flavor to add variety). OR Zevia Soda (Black Cherry, Cream Soda, Ginger Root beer, Orange, Strawberry, Cola, etc)

Directions: Mix Protein Powder with water, ice and stevia in blender. OR mix protein powder in 1-2 oz water, ice and add soda.
Makes 1 serving (1 fruit)

Raw Apple Sauce

Ingredients
1 apple sliced
1/2 teaspoon cinnamon
Pinch of nutmeg
Powdered stevia or liquid vanilla stevia to taste

Directions: Peel and puree apple in food processor. Add cinnamon and stevia to taste.
Makes 1 serving (1 fruit)

Strawberries or Orange Slices dipped in Dark Chocolate

Ingredients
1 orange, peeled and sliced or handful of strawberries sliced
Dark chocolate stevia extract

Directions: Arrange orange or strawberry slices in a bowl. Drizzle dark chocolate stevia over the slices and serve chilled. You can use any stevia flavor! Add slivered almonds for a treat! Makes 1 serving (1 fruit)

Warm Berry Medley

Ingredients

1 cup Blackberries
1 cup Raspberries
1 cup Strawberries
Any combo of berries
Powdered stevia (or honey) to taste
Variation: 1/2 cup old fashioned oats
1/2 cup Just Almond Meal (Trader Joes)
1/4 tsp vanilla stevia
1/3 cup MCT oil
3/4 tsp cinnamon
1/4 tsp sea salt

Directions: Spray MCT oil in 8 x 8 x 2 baking dish and layer berries and sprinkle with powdered stevia. Bake in 350 oven for about 20 minutes. Enjoy warm or sprinkle over whole Greek yogurt. Variation: On maintenance diet mix vanilla stevia, oats, almond meal, oil, cinnamon & salt. Sprinkle topping over stevia-free berries in baking dish and bake in 375 for about 30 minutes, until topping is light brown and fruit is bubbling. I sometimes put a little half and half over dessert or add some crushed almonds to mixture for a little more crunch. Makes 6 servings (1 fruit)

Warm Spiced Oranges

Ingredients
One orange sliced or segmented
2 tablespoons lemon juice
1/8 teaspoon ground cinnamon
Dash of cloves
Dash of nutmeg
1/8 teaspoon powdered vanilla
Stevia to taste (powdered or flavored liquid)

Directions: Mix spices with lemon juice and stevia. Warm slightly in saucepan and add oranges. Cook for 2-3 minutes. Serve hot or chilled.
Makes 1 serving (1 fruit)

Dana Luchini has been in the health and beauty industry for over 20 years as a Medical Esthetician & Certified Nutritional Therapist. She combines internal & external healthy-aging skin & body solutions, which include the prescription HCG **Healthy-Aging Diet™** Weight Loss Program and the latest organic anti-aging skin care options for rejuvenating and maintaining healthy skin & body.

Healthy Aging Diet™
&
Healthy Aging Body™

Wellness & Weight Loss Clinics

2 Convenient Locations in WA

Tacoma: *Healthy Aging Diet®*
1310 S. Union, Bldg A, Ste 3A, Tacoma, WA. 98405
Ph: 253-272-4244 Fax: 253-272-4448
www.HealthyagingDiet.com

Spokane: *Healthy Aging Body™*
3131 North Division, Suite 201, Spokane, WA. 99207
Ph: 509-324-0444 or 855-429-DIET (3438) Fax: 509-324-4244
www.HealthyAgingBody.com

©2012 by Dana Luchini **ALL Rights Reserved.**
First print edition 07.27.2012   Third print edition 11/11/12   ISBN- 13:9781480298330
No part of this book may be reproduced, stored in a retrieval system, or transmitted by any means: electronic, mechanical, photocopying, recording or otherwise, without written permission from the author.

This Book is printed in the USA

Made in the USA
Charleston, SC
09 September 2013